The Circle of Growth

A practical leadership operating system

Written by

THEODORE *Teddy Bear* SCHIELE

Copyright © 2025

The Circle of Growth: **A practical leadership operating system**

LCCN 2025922337

eBook – 979-8-90046-738-2

Paperback - 979-8-90046-741-2

Publisher - Staten House

All Rights Reserved. Any unauthorized reprinting or use of this material is strictly prohibited. No part of this book may be reproduced or transmitted in any form or by any means, electronic or mechanical, including photocopying, recording, or by any information storage and retrieval system without express written permission from the author. All reasonable attempts have been made to verify the accuracy of the information provided in this publication. Nevertheless, the author assumes no responsibility.

The Circle of Growth — A practical leadership operating system

Table of Contents

The Circle of Growth — 1

Part I — 1
- Foundations of Growth — 1
- Why I Built the Circle of Growth — 2
- Interlude: The Journey I — New Map, Same Town — 3
- What Is "Scalable Growth"? — 20
- Avoiding the "iPerson" Trap — 21
- Visionary or Implementer — 23

Part II — 25
- The Growth Grid — 25
- Interlude: The Journey II — Proof Before Spotlight — 26
- The Growth Grid — 47
- How You're Wired to Grow — 47
- Circle of Growth Mantra — 49

Part III — 50
- The Three Stages of Growth — 50
- Interlude — 51
- The Journey III — Trial by Clarity — 51
- Stages of Growth — 65
- The Adversity Zone — the second stage of growth, where comfort ends and character starts. — 68
- The Zone of Growth — where purpose becomes your pattern. — 72

Part IV	75
Leadership Operating System	75
Interlude: The Journey IV — Context Over Clout	76
Part V	95
Scaling Growth	95
Interlude: The Journey V — How the Leader Operating System works	96
Personal Growth	106
Professional Development	108
Scaling Growth Through S.U.M. — *The Visionary Builder*	113
The Asset Navigator — *Scaling From Builder to Strategic Investor*	117
Conclusion	124
Light the Loop	124
Light the Loop – Field Guide	125
The Loop: Your New Leadership Rhythm	125
The 7 Traits: Who You Are	132
The 7 Actions: What You Do	138
The 7 Ps: Where It Applies (Focus Areas)	145
S.U.M.: Scaling Up (System, Unity, Mastery)	153
Circle of Growth Cheat Sheet (One-Page Blueprint)	160
Thinkers, Operators, and Frameworks That Sharpened the Circle	164
Glossary	187
A	187

B	188
C	188
D	191
E	191
F	193
G	194
H	195
I	195
L	197
M	198
O	199
P	201
R	203
S	203
T	205
U	206
V	207
Z	208
Discussion Prompts for *The Circle of Growth*	209
The Seven Actions of the Growth Loop	209
The Seven Traits (Who You Are as a Leader)	210
The Growth Grid (Finding Your Natural Lane)	211
Adversity to Growth Model (Comfort Zone → Adversity Zone → Growth Zone)	212
The Seven Ps (Key Focus Areas of the System)	213

The S.U.M. Culture Model (Scaling Up: System, Unity, Mastery) 214

The Asset Navigator Framework (From Builder to Investor) 215

Acknowledgments 215

Executive Summary

A Framework for Real Growth

The *Circle of Growth* is not a theory or a pep talk—it's a leadership operating system. It's designed for anyone serious about turning purpose into performance, whether you're running a business, leading a team, or simply trying to become more effective in your own life. It's built around one core belief: *systems beat circumstances.*

The system connects who you are to what you do. Every chapter, every story, and every tool in this book serves that purpose—to help you turn clarity into action, action into results, and results into momentum. It's about building the kind of growth that lasts because it's rooted in character, discipline, and rhythm.

At its heart, the Circle of Growth runs on a loop: **Assess → Clarify → Harness → Innovate → Empower → Validate → Execute.** Each stage strengthens the next. It's not a one-time climb—it's a cycle of continual improvement. When you run this loop with intention, you create predictable progress without burning out, guessing, or losing integrity along the way.

Why the Circle Exists

The world doesn't fail for lack of ideas—it fails for lack of systems. Most leaders know what they want to achieve but don't have a clear way to get there. Meetings fill calendars, projects lose direction, and culture becomes a slogan instead of a standard. The Circle of Growth exists to fix that.

It gives you a structured rhythm—a leadership operating system—that makes clarity, accountability, and alignment daily habits instead of yearly goals. It helps you find your bearings when life or business gets chaotic, because the same principles that make a company work also make a person effective: truth first, clarity next, execution always.

This isn't just for executives. It's written for the builder trying to keep a dream alive, the manager learning to lead with both empathy and precision, and the entrepreneur realizing hustle alone doesn't scale. The Circle of Growth meets you where you are and gives you a repeatable path forward.

The Foundation: Scalable Growth

Real growth isn't hype—it's structure. Scalable growth means you can keep winning without losing your sanity or your soul. It's the kind of growth that compounds instead of collapsing.

In practical terms, it looks like this:

- You stop chasing one-off wins and start building repeatable wins.

- You replace heroic effort with healthy rhythm.

- You shift from surviving emergencies to running on systems.

Every part of your life or business—your habits, relationships, and results—should be able to withstand pressure and still perform. The Circle helps you build scaffolding strong enough to hold your success, not just your ambition.

Growth that lasts is built like a house, not a headline: brick by brick, truth by truth, loop by loop.

The Growth Journey: From Comfort to Capacity

Growth happens in three predictable zones:

1. **The Comfort Zone** – It feels safe, familiar, and low-risk. But it's not peace—it's paralysis with good branding. Comfort keeps you busy without progress. You stay where it's easy and wonder why nothing changes.

2. **The Adversity Zone** – The paper-cut stage of growth. This is where friction and failure test you. It's where self-doubt shouts loudest and where excuses are loud but optional. The secret is not to escape adversity but to outlast it with rhythm, reflection, and repetition.

3. **The Zone of Growth** – The reward for staying in the fight. It's not a finish line—it's a rhythm. You start to recover faster, lead with calm, and operate from peace instead of panic. Growth stops feeling dramatic and starts feeling normal.

The book teaches that comfort is a cage, adversity is a teacher, and growth is a choice you make every day. Every cycle of the Circle builds capacity, confidence, and clarity.

The Operating System: Leadership in Motion

Leadership is not a title; it's a rhythm. The Circle of Growth provides seven core **traits** and seven corresponding **actions** that create measurable leadership.

Traits (Who You Are):

- **Self-Awareness** – See yourself clearly so you can lead yourself honestly.

- **Courage** – Choose action and truth over comfort and silence.

- **Humility** – Stay teachable and put the mission before your ego.

- **Integrity** – Align your values with your behavior, even when it costs you.

- **Empathy** – Lead people, not positions. Understand before you manage.

- **Learning** – Treat every mistake as data. Curiosity beats pride every time.

- **Execution** – Finish what you start, consistently and well.

Actions (What You Do):

1. **Assess** – Tell the truth about where you are.

2. **Clarify** – Define success in plain language.

3. **Harness** – Focus your people and energy where it matters.

4. **Innovate** – Find smarter, values-aligned ways to improve.

5. **Empower** – Delegate, trust, and develop others.

6. **Validate** – Measure real progress and learn from the data.

7. **Execute** – Deliver results reliably—no hype, no half-finish.

When your traits and actions align, you get traction. Your character becomes visible in your calendar.

The 7 Ps: Where the Work Happens

The Circle of Growth runs across seven arenas—the "7 Ps." Together they form the blueprint for sustainable success:

- **Purpose:** The "why" behind what you do.

- **People:** The who—your team, relationships, and trust.

- **Product:** The value you deliver.

- **Process:** The systems that keep you efficient and consistent.

- **Principles:** The ethical guardrails that preserve integrity.

- **Performance:** The results and metrics that prove progress.

- **Profit:** The sustainable outcomes that fuel the next loop.

When these seven are aligned, your organization—and your life—move as one integrated system.

S.U.M.: Scaling the System

Once you master the loop personally, the next challenge is scaling it. *S.U.M.*—System, Unity, Mastery—is how growth becomes culture.

- **System:** Build structures that reward truth, teamwork, and consistency. Make collaboration the easiest path to success.

- **Unity:** Create shared rhythms—meetings, rituals, and cadences—so everyone stays aligned and informed.

- **Mastery:** Share knowledge openly. Teach what you learn. Build bench strength so no one person is a single point of failure.

When S.U.M. is in place, leadership no longer depends on charisma—it runs on cadence. The organization grows even when the founder rests.

The Growth Grid: Know Your Lane

Not everyone grows the same way. The Growth Grid helps you identify how you're wired so you can lead in alignment with your nature:

- **Contributor:** Steady, structured, reliable. You bring order and consistency.

- **Independent Creator:** Entrepreneurial, driven, innovative. You thrive on autonomy.

- **Visionary Builder:** Big-picture thinker who scales ideas into systems.

- **Strategic Investor:** Long-term thinker who multiplies impact through ownership and capital.

Knowing your lane helps you stop forcing a life that doesn't fit and start building one that does. Growth accelerates when effort matches design.

The Asset Navigator: From Builder to Investor
The final stage of growth is stewardship—learning to make your capital, influence, and knowledge work as hard as you did. The *Asset Navigator* transforms leaders into strategic investors.

You move from doing the work to designing systems that do the work. You begin to:

- Align your wealth with your values.

- Turn lessons into assets.

- Mentor others to carry your vision forward.

- Build legacy through systems, not slogans.

Wealth—of time, resources, and impact—is no longer something you chase; it's something your systems produce.

The Vision: Proof Over Polish
The Circle of Growth stands for one simple truth: results built on proof outlast those built on polish. Leaders don't need more motivation; they need more rhythm—habits that link who they are to what gets done.

Every story in this book—from Yeshua's quiet rise out of complacency to the way teams handled chaos at a farmers' market—

teaches the same principle: clarity beats chaos, systems beat circumstance, and consistency beats talent.

Growth isn't about being fearless—it's about being faithful. It's about showing up, running the loop, and keeping your word when it's hard.

The Invitation: Light the Loop

If you only read this summary, let this part stay with you: your growth is a system, not a secret.

Run the loop. Start small. Tell the truth. Act on purpose. Build systems that protect your momentum. Teach others how to do the same.

Because in leadership, as in life, the real measure isn't how much you start—it's how well you finish, how often you repeat, and how faithfully you build.

The Circle of Growth is your playbook for doing exactly that:
Purpose as the point. Intent as the engine. Systems as the difference.

Run the loop—and keep lighting it, one cycle at a time.

Download the Circle of Growth Illustrated Guide
Get the full, graphics-based *Circle of Growth* informational — complete with clear visuals and diagrams that bring each stage of growth to life. Perfect for teams, presentations, and quick reference

About the Author

"I don't take **leadership advice** from people born on first base or handed the keys. I started at zero, built wealth, lost it, and built it again—not from luck, from a system. *Systems* beat *circumstances*. If you want wins without a head start, learn from scars, not shortcuts. I'll give you the playbook."

— Theodore "**Teddy Bear**" Schiele

I started at zero in Ferriday, Louisiana—more grit than guidance, more bills than answers. The military shaped my backbone; entrepreneurship sharpened my playbook. Over 24 years in the U.S. Army National Guard, I learned to lead under pressure, earn trust, and keep the mission first. In business, I learned that systems beat circumstances. That conviction became **the Circle of Growth**™—a practical loop that aligns who you are with what you consistently deliver.

Today, as a Leadership Consultant, Business Growth Strategist, and author, I help leaders and organizations compound results through clarity, systems, and legacy-driven leadership. My firm, **Schiele & Associates,** provides strategic planning, capability building, and in-the-trenches implementation so transformation doesn't stall at the whiteboard. We work where character meets cadence: from operating rhythms and goal systems to culture, coaching, and execution you can audit.

My philosophy is simple:

- **Purpose is the point.**
- **Intent is the engine.**
- **Systems make it repeatable.**

I created **the Circle of Growth**™ to turn values into patterns, patterns into culture, and culture into outcomes. The work serves boardrooms and underserved communities alike—because opportunity compounds fastest where knowledge and access finally meet. I've helped nonprofits raise more, founders scale smarter, and executives lead with humility, courage, and measurable discipline.

Legacy Tools — End-of-Book Essentials

1. **References & Bibliography**
   Thinkers, operators, and frameworks that sharpened the Circle.

2. **Appendices (Field Kits)**
   Diagrams, scorecards, journaling prompts, and step-by-step exercises.

3. **Glossary**
   Plain-English definitions so teams align before executing.

4. **Further Reading**
   Curated books, articles, and voices to extend the journey.

5. **Book Club & Leadership Circle Discussion Questions**
   Prompts for teams, classrooms, and cohorts.

6. **Acknowledgments**

Welcome to Circle of Growth:
A Practical Leadership Operating System.

This book is your entry point into a framework designed to transform potential into performance—without the fluff. Whether you're leading a team, building a business, or recalibrating your direction, this system meets you where you are and moves you forward with clarity, accountability, and traction. Expect a no-nonsense approach to leadership that's actionable, human-centered, and built to scale. Let's cut through the noise and start building momentum that lasts.

Part I

Foundations of Growth

Why I Built the Circle of Growth

A Playbook for the "Make You / Break You" Years

This isn't just for one lane. It works for the new manager trying not to drown in meetings, the nonprofit founder building impact with limited resources, the executive aligning a messy org chart, and the veteran translating discipline into civilian momentum. It works for anyone tired of motivational quotes with no muscle behind them. You don't need a perfect plan—you need a repeatable rhythm that upgrades your habits one notch at a time.

So if these years feel loud and direction feels quiet, welcome. **The Circle of Growth** won't promise easy—but it will give you a path. Not theory. Not vibes. A real operating system for your life. Run the loop, win small, repeat. That's how these years make you—not break you.

Interlude: The Journey I — New Map, Same Town

Yeshua Mateo wipes down the last cracked vinyl booth at Rosie's Diner as dusk settles over the one-stoplight town. Outside the plate-glass window, Main Street lies empty, bathed in the orange glow of a lone streetlamp. Inside, two old-timers nurse their coffees at the counter, voices low and gruff. Yeshua half-listens as he works, absorbing their ritual end-of-day grumbling.

"Town ain't what it used to be," groans Earl, tapping a sugar packet against the Formica counter. "Kids these days all runnin' off to the city or wasting time on their phones. No grit no more."

His companion, Dale, snorts in agreement. "Yup. No gratitude neither. I gave thirty years to the mill, and for what? So some hotshot outta college could shut it down." He shakes his head, bitterness thick in his voice.

Yeshua tenses at their words, **feeling that low-grade negativity hang in the air like stale cigarette smoke.** He knows the men don't mean him specifically, but each complaint lands heavy. At twenty-two, Yeshua has heard it all before – *nothing changes, nobody cares, why even try*. In a town this small, dreams often feel like antiques gathering dust.

He quietly flips the chairs onto the tabletops, one by one. The routine is muscle memory by now, yet tonight his mind wanders. Through the window, he catches a glimpse of headlights from the 8:40 intercity bus as it rumbles past the diner and disappears into the twilight. Every night he watches that bus come and go, and every night something inside him aches to be on it. *One day*, he thinks, *one day I'll buy a ticket and just leave.* The thought is both thrilling and terrifying. He presses a palm against the cool glass for a moment, watching the red taillights glow and fade. In their fleeting light, he sees his reflection – a tall, lean young man with tired eyes and an apron stained with coffee and grease. A young man who, if he's honest, feels *stuck*.

He forces himself back to the task at hand. There's comfort in the small things he can control, like leaving each table clean and each salt shaker filled. As he wipes the last table, he overhears Earl mutter behind him, "That Mateo kid's still here, huh? Thought he'd have skedaddled like the rest of 'em by now." Earl's voice isn't unkind, more puzzled.

Dale chuckles. "Yeshua? Nah, that boy's loyal to this place. Probably end up managing Rosie's when Frank retires."

Yeshua's grip tightens on the damp rag. The idea of still being here in five years makes his stomach sink. He doesn't want to disrespect the diner – it's honest work – but **he quietly fears a life where *every* tomorrow looks just like today.**

At that moment, the kitchen door swings open and Frank, the diner's owner, steps out, wiping his hands on his apron. "Closing time, gentlemen," Frank calls to the regulars. He's a heavyset man with thinning hair and a permanent frown etched on his face. "Finish up, I gotta close the till."

Earl and Dale toss bills on the counter and shuffle out with a wave. "Night, Yeshua," Earl offers. Yeshua nods politely, managing a small smile.

"Night, Mr. Earl. Get home safe." The bell over the door jingles as they exit, leaving the diner suddenly silent.

Frank eyes Yeshua and the half-cleaned floor. "Make sure you mop up proper. Last Friday you missed a spot under the corner booth," he says, voice flat. No praise for the spotless tables or the double shift Yeshua pulled, just the usual prickly critique.

Yeshua swallows the reflex to defend his work. "Yes, sir. I'll make sure it's done right," he replies evenly. He's long learned that arguing with Frank is as pointless as scrubbing a mud-stained floor with a dry sponge. Frank always has to have the last word.

From behind the counter, a light female voice pipes up. "I already mixed the mop water, Yeshua. I can finish that up." It's Eliza, standing by the bucket and wringer. She flashes him an empathetic smile. Tonight is her last shift at Rosie's – tomorrow she leaves for college in Chicago, a world far beyond this town's limits.

"You sure, El?" Yeshua asks, grateful.

She nods. "Least I can do on my last day." Eliza casts a wary glance at Frank, who is hunched over the register counting cash. Lowering her voice, she adds, "Plus, I think you could use a breather."

Yeshua doesn't need convincing. He unties his apron and hangs it on the hook. "Thanks. I'll go take out the trash in back." It's an excuse to step outside for air, but also to give Eliza a moment alone with Frank. He suspects she plans to talk to the old man before she leaves for good.

Outside, night has settled. The summer air is warm and humming with crickets. Yeshua breathes deeply, inhaling the scent of fried onions and asphalt – the smell of closing time. He hauls the trash bag into the dumpster, then lingers, stretching the ache from his shoulders. Above, a few stars peek out where the purple sky darkens.

From inside the diner, muffled voices trickle through the propped-open back door. Eliza and Frank – their words indistinct. He hears Frank's gruff mumble and Eliza's gentle tone responding. It sounds like she's thanking him for the job, and maybe… yes, there it is. Frank's voice cracks just a little. "…You take care, kid," Yeshua hears.

Moments later, Eliza pushes through the back door, wiping a tear from her eye. She forces a smile. "Well, that's that."

Yeshua tilts his head. "You okay?"

She nods, holding up a small envelope. "Frank actually gave me a recommendation letter and a hundred bucks as a going-away bonus. Can you believe it?"

Yeshua can't hide his surprise. "Frank did that? Maybe he's a softie deep down."

Eliza laughs, a bright sound in the dark alley. "Deep, *deep* down," she agrees. They share a grin. For all Frank's rough edges, he did right by Eliza in the end.

They walk to the front of the diner, where Frank has already locked up and departed. On the sidewalk, the neon **ROSIE'S** sign buzzes faintly. Eliza takes off her apron and folds it neatly, a symbolic gesture of closure. Yeshua watches her, heart heavy and hopeful all at once.

"You really did it," he says softly. "You're getting out of here."

Eliza slings her backpack over her shoulder. "We did it together. You covered so many of my shifts when I was studying for SATs and working on applications. I couldn't have managed without you."

He shakes his head. "All I did was flip pancakes and refill coffee."

"And encourage me when I wanted to give up," she adds, touching his arm. "Don't downplay it, Yeshua. You always believed I could do more... even when I didn't believe it myself."

Yeshua shrugs, a little embarrassed. "Of course I did. You're going to shine up there in Chicago, El." He means it. Eliza is smart, kind, bound for bigger things than wiping tables in Briarcliff (their town's humble name, seldom seen on any map).

They start walking down the empty street, past darkened storefronts that haven't changed since they were kids. Their footsteps echo against brick buildings. The only open shop is the gas station at the corner, its fluorescent light flickering. Yeshua's truck is parked under a pecan tree where the diner lot meets the road. He offers to drive Eliza home.

In the cab of the old pickup, they sit for a moment with the engine off. Neither seems to want the night to end. Eliza gazes out the window at the quiet street. "I'm excited, but I'm scared too," she admits in a rare moment of vulnerability. "Everything will be so new, and I keep thinking… what if I don't belong up there?"

Yeshua turns the key, and the truck rumbles to life. "You'll belong," he says firmly as he pulls onto the road. "That place is lucky to have you. You'll make friends in no time, join all those college clubs you talked about… It'll be great."

She smiles, but there's worry in it. "What about you? I hate the thought of leaving you behind. You're my best friend, Yeshua."

He grips the wheel, unsure how to answer. A part of him wants to blurt out *Don't worry, I'll follow soon!* But he isn't sure if that's true or just a comforting fantasy. "I'll be fine," he says after a pause. "I've got some things to figure out here, but… I'll be fine."

They both know life is pulling them in different directions. The truck rolls past the darkened high school and the shuttered movie theater. These streets hold a thousand memories: summer bike races, football pep rallies, the spot by the water tower where they used to sneak sodas and talk about their dreams. At a red light, Yeshua notices Eliza studying him.

"You deserve more than this, you know," she says suddenly.

"More than what?" he asks, though he knows exactly what she means.

She gestures vaguely at the silent town. "*This.* Staying here because it's safe. Working yourself to the bone for people like Frank, who barely say thanks. You have talent, Yeshua. You're creative, you care about people... I just don't want to see you settle."

He doesn't reply at first. In his chest, a mix of pride and shame churns. Pride because her belief in him buoys him; shame because deep down he wonders if he *has* been hiding here out of fear. "It's not that simple," he finally says quietly as the light turns green. "Not everyone gets opportunities, El. College... traveling... I wouldn't even know where to start."

Eliza reaches over and gently squeezes his arm. "Just promise me you'll try. Apply for that design apprenticeship you told me about, or talk to Coach Barnes about the community college. Something. Anything. Just don't give up on your dreams."

Yeshua's throat tightens. They've had versions of this conversation before, but this farewell makes it painfully real. "I promise I'll try," he whispers, unable to find a louder voice.

They pull up in front of Eliza's house – a small bungalow with peeling paint that looks ghostly in the streetlight. She unbuckles her seatbelt slowly. "Will you come see me off tomorrow?"

He forces a smile. "Try and stop me. Bus leaves at 8, right?"

"8 AM sharp," she confirms. She hesitates, then throws her arms around him in a tight hug. Yeshua returns it, swallowing hard against the lump in his throat.

"Thank you, for everything," she murmurs.

"Thank *you*," he replies, voice barely above a breath. "Go do big things, El."

When she pulls back, her eyes glisten with tears she won't let fall. With a final smile, Eliza climbs out of the truck. Yeshua waits until she's safely inside her house before driving off, his heart heavier than the humid night air.

On the ride home, he rolls down the window, hoping the wind might clear his mind. Instead, memories flood in – Eliza and him at age ten, scheming about arcade games; at sixteen, when she beat him on an algebra test and teased him for weeks; last year, when her college acceptance letter arrived and they'd jumped around her living room in joy. He was genuinely happy for her... and yet tonight, he can't escape the ache of being left behind.

He parks outside the small duplex where he lives with his mom. The lights are off; she's likely asleep, exhausted from her nursing shift. Yeshua quietly slips inside. In the glow of the stove's night-light, he scribbles a quick note and leaves it on the kitchen counter: *Took out trash & cleaned up. Get some rest, Ma. Love you.* He doesn't want to wake her at this late hour.

In his tiny bedroom, Yeshua collapses onto the bed without even changing out of his diner uniform. Through the thin walls, he can hear the neighbor's TV and the distant whistle of a freight train. He lies there staring at the ceiling fan slowly rotating, stirring the warm air. **Doubt creeps in, whispering that he's running out of time to become anything more than "the Mateo kid" working the diner.**

He reaches under his bed and pulls out a shoebox he hasn't opened in months. Inside are pamphlets and printouts – a tech boot camp flyer, an application for a graphic design internship in the city, notes he took at a free community workshop on starting a business. Each item represents a road not taken, an idea that excited him before he buried it under excuses. He thumbs through them, guilt and longing twisting inside.

One crumpled flyer catches his eye: a leadership seminar series that had come through the next town over last year. He'd jotted down one of the speaker's lines: **"If you keep waiting for the right time, you'll wake up one day and realize it passed you by."** He had underlined it twice. At the time, he felt seen by those words, fired up even. But then the daily grind swallowed him back up, and nothing changed.

Yeshua closes the box, determination and frustration battling within him. In the silence he admits a hard truth: *he* is the one holding himself back. Not the town, not lack of money or connections – those are challenges, but the real barrier has been his own fear of failure, his own comfortable routines. It's a bitter pill to swallow. He runs a hand through his dark hair and sits up.

Looking at the closed box at his feet, he makes a quiet vow: "No more waiting." Saying it aloud makes it feel real. Tomorrow, after he sees Eliza off, he'll start taking steps – however small – toward a different life. With that resolve easing his mind, Yeshua finally drifts to sleep, the chirp of crickets lulling him into dreams of unfamiliar cities and open roads.

Morning comes sooner than expected. Yeshua wakes to his phone alarm blaring at 6:30 AM. For a moment, he considers sleeping in – it's his day off at the diner – but memory rushes back: Eliza's bus. He promised to be there. He throws on clean jeans and a worn navy t-shirt and splashes water on his face, skipping breakfast to avoid being late.

The old pickup coughs to life in the dewy morning, and Yeshua speeds toward the Greyhound stop on the edge of town. The rising sun paints the sky in hues of pink and gold, far prettier than one might expect in a place so ordinary. He arrives with minutes to spare. The bus is already parked, engine idling, a few passengers boarding.

Eliza stands by her parents near the curb, hugging them tightly. Her duffel bag and suitcase rest at her feet. Yeshua hangs back for a moment, not wanting to intrude on their family goodbye. He watches as her mother brushes a tear from Eliza's cheek and her father, arms crossed to hide his emotion, nods gruffly at something Eliza says. Despite the solemnity, there's pride in their faces.

When Eliza spots Yeshua, her face lights up. She waves him over enthusiastically. "You made it!" she calls.

He grins, jogging up. "Of course. I wouldn't let you leave without saying a proper goodbye."

Eliza's dad pats Yeshua on the back. "Take care of yourself, son. And thank you for looking out for our girl all these years."

"Yes, thank you, Yeshua," her mom adds softly, eyes kind.

Yeshua shuffles, a bit embarrassed by the attention. "I–it was nothing, really. Eliza did all the hard work."

They insist on a quick group photo – Eliza in the middle, flanked by her parents, with Yeshua standing just beside her. Her mom fumbles with her phone camera until Yeshua gently takes it and offers to snap the picture so the whole family can be in it. After a few tries, they succeed – Eliza holding up a peace sign, trying to smile through impending tears.

The bus driver honks lightly, signaling final boarding. Eliza's parents give her one more round of hugs and step back. Then Eliza turns to Yeshua, and the rest of the world seems to blur for a moment. She throws her arms around him just as she did the night before, only this time she doesn't hold back the tears. He feels them damp on his shoulder.

"Promise me you'll keep that promise," she whispers fiercely.

He knows what she means: the promise to try, to pursue something more. Yeshua nods, his own eyes burning. "I will. I promise."

She pulls back, hands on his shoulders as if memorizing his face. "Text me, call me, *anything* if you need to talk. I'll be back to visit at Thanksgiving, okay? That's not so far."

"Okay," he manages to say. They both know it feels like an eternity right now, but he forces a smile. "Go on, they're waiting for you."

With a final trembling breath, Eliza picks up her duffel and boards the bus. Yeshua and her parents stand together, waving as she finds a window seat. Eliza presses a hand to the glass in a little wave. Yeshua does the same.

The bus doors hiss shut. In a belch of diesel fumes, the Greyhound pulls away. Eliza's face remains at the window until the bus turns the corner and is gone, leaving only an empty road and the three of them staring after it.

Her father clears his throat, blinking hard. "Well... time to get on then," he murmurs, mustering a smile for his wife. They thank Yeshua again and invite him to dinner next week, "so the house doesn't feel so empty," her mom says with a sad smile. He promises to come by, and they depart.

Yeshua remains on the curb a moment longer, the morning quiet around him. He feels small and solitary now. Taking a deep breath, he closes his eyes. **He can almost see it – a fork in the road ahead, one path safe and familiar, the other unknown and frightening.** His heart beats in his ears as he makes a choice.

Climbing back into his pickup, Yeshua pulls out his phone. Before he can overthink it, he taps open the email app and hits "Compose." The blank screen stares back. He types out a message to the contact listed on that design apprenticeship flyer – the one he'd hidden in the shoebox. It's a long shot, months past the deadline, but maybe they have another program or could keep him in mind. He pours sincerity into a short paragraph expressing his interest in any opportunity to learn and work hard. After a final glance, he presses send. A surge of relief and adrenaline washes over him – a small step, but a step at last.

Next, he opens a draft message addressed to Coach Barnes, the community college advisor and an old mentor from high school. Yeshua asks about upcoming classes or programs in business or technology, mentioning he's thinking of enrolling. He promises to follow up in person soon. He hits send on that too. Each email sent feels like cracking open a window in a stuffy room. Fresh possibilities drift in.

As he starts the truck, Yeshua notices his hands trembling slightly on the wheel. Part excitement, part fear. He just set things in motion; there's no taking it back. The old doubts try to surface – *What if I'm too late? What if I fail?* – but he steels himself. **"When ego runs the show, nothing new can get in,"** he recalls someone saying. And he finally understands. If he clings to pride or fear of looking foolish, he'll never learn anything new, never grow. He refuses to let that happen.

Instead of driving straight home, Yeshua finds himself heading toward the diner. He isn't due in today, but something tells him he needs to do one more hard thing before he loses his nerve. As he parks out front, the morning rush is in full swing. Through the window he sees Frank barking orders at a junior waitress and the cook flipping eggs on the griddle. Normally, on a day off, Yeshua would avoid this place. But not today.

He steps inside, weaving through the familiar chaos of clattering dishes and percolating coffee. Frank spots him and scowls in confusion. "Mateo, what're you doing here? You're off Thursdays."

"I know," Yeshua says, finding strength in his steady tone. "Can we talk for a minute, boss?"

Frank grunts, clearly irritated but curious enough. He jerks his head toward the back office. Yeshua follows him past the swinging kitchen door. His heart thumps wildly, but his mind is oddly calm.

In the cramped office, amid stacks of invoices and the faint smell of bacon grease, Frank crosses his arms. "Make it quick, I got a diner full of customers."

Yeshua takes a breath. "Sir, I want to thank you for everything you've taught me here. I've grown a lot working for you these past few years."

Frank raises an eyebrow at the unexpected gratitude. "Uh, sure. You've been a good worker. One of the best, actually." It sounds grudging, but genuine.

Yeshua musters a small smile. Coming from Frank, that's high praise. "That means a lot to me." He straightens his shoulders. "Which is why it's hard for me to say this… but I need to give you my notice. Two weeks from now, I'll be moving on."

Frank's eyes widen. For a moment he just studies Yeshua, as if unsure he heard right. "You quitting, kid?"

"Yes." Yeshua's voice stays calm and firm. "It's time I try something different. Maybe college, maybe an apprenticeship in the city. I'm not entirely sure yet, but I have to find out."

Frank's face hardens; defensiveness creeps into his tone. "Is this about money? I know I can't pay what some big city joint would, but this is steady work. Your daddy had a job here when he was your age, didn't do him wrong."

"It's not about the money," Yeshua replies quickly. He's grateful Frank gave him a job when he needed one. This isn't about that. "It's about… my future. I don't want to look back in ten years and realize I never left my comfort zone."

Frank scratches his balding head, struggling to process. He's not an emotional man, and Yeshua can see him wrestling between annoyance and a hint of respect. "You think you're too good for diner life now? That it?"

The bite in his words stings, but Yeshua stands his ground, shaking his head. "No, sir. I don't think I'm *too good* for anything. I just want to see what I'm capable of. I can't do that if I stay here forever."

Frank's jaw works side to side. Yeshua has seen him chew out truckers for less, but now the old man just looks... conflicted. "Damn, kid. You and Eliza both. Must be somethin' in the water, huh?" He tries to joke, but it falls flat. An awkward silence stretches.

Finally, Frank nods gruffly. "Alright. Two weeks. But let me give you a piece of advice before you run off chasing something: The world out there," he jabs a thumb toward the window, "it doesn't care about you like folks do here. You might find it's not so friendly beyond Briarcliff."

Yeshua meets his gaze steadily. "I know it won't be easy. But I have to find my own way."

Frank squints, then snorts. "You got that stubborn look your father used to get. Once Mateo men set their mind, wild horses can't drag 'em." It's the closest Frank has come to complimenting Yeshua's resolve.

Yeshua offers his hand. "Thank you, Frank. For everything."

Frank looks at the outstretched hand, then clasps it in a firm shake. "You come back if things don't pan out, hear? I'll leave a spot on the grill for you."

A swell of gratitude rushes through Yeshua. "I appreciate that. Truly."

He turns to leave, but Frank's voice halts him. "Hey."

Yeshua glances back. The older man clears his throat, avoiding eye contact. "Proud of you, kid. Don't expect me to say it again, but... yeah. Go do good."

Emotion catches Yeshua off guard. He nods, a smile breaking free. "I will. Thank you."

Stepping out of the office, Yeshua feels a weight lift off his shoulders. The rush of the diner seems muted now, as if the noise and sizzle no longer tether him. He walks out into the bright morning light, blinking at the clarity of the day.

On the sidewalk, he pauses and inhales deeply. The air even smells different – full of possibility. He looks down the road to where it disappears over the gentle hill leading out of town. The world beyond is unknown, yes, but at this moment he feels something unexpected stirring within: hope.

Yeshua pulls out his phone and shoots off a quick text to Eliza: *"Gave my notice at Rosie's. Your turn to be proud of me. ☐"* He hits send, imagining her surprise and excitement when she sees it later.

Tossing the phone into his truck, he doesn't start the engine right away. Instead, he leans against the hood and just stands there, face turned toward the horizon. He allows himself a rare moment of pride. For the first time, he chose uncertainty over regret. It feels like the beginning of *something*.

He didn't need to win an argument with anyone; he needed to win back his life. And by choosing to step away from what was safe, he already has. Yeshua knows there will be challenges ahead – new faces, new failures, maybe even a formidable antagonist or two waiting down the road (he's heard enough stories to know not everyone will wish him well). But that's alright. He's taken the first step, and right now the morning sun on his face feels like a quiet celebration of that courage.

Climbing into the truck, Yeshua finally heads home to plan his next moves. As he drives, he catches his reflection once more in the rearview mirror. There's a spark in his eyes he hasn't seen before. The journey has begun, and he isn't on it alone – he carries with him the hopes of his friends, the lessons from his town, and a budding faith in himself.

In the days to come, Yeshua Mateo will meet allies and adversaries, face tests of character and will. But today, on this humble morning, he allows himself a triumphant grin. He imagines Eliza cheering in delight at his news. He imagines his future friends – whoever they are – out there waiting to cross paths with him. And he imagines, just briefly, the face of a rival he has yet to encounter: someone who will challenge everything he's learning about humility and growth. The thought no longer scares him; in fact, it steels his resolve.

Yeshua turns on the radio and hums along as the truck ambles down the road. He doesn't know exactly where that road will lead, but for the first time in his life, he's eager to find out. **Real growth, he reminds himself, is simple math: reflection → adjustment → progress.** He's done the reflecting. He's making the adjustment. Now, it's time to chase progress – one mile at a time.

As Briarcliff's city limits fade in his rearview, Yeshua whispers a quiet goodbye to the boy who doubted and a grateful hello to the young man emerging. The journey – *his* journey – is just getting started. And he can't wait for what comes next.

What Is "Scalable Growth"?

Here's the truth without the varnish: real growth isn't a highlight reel. It's scaffolding. If it can't hold your weight on a random Tuesday, it's not growth—it's a moment. Scalable growth is the kind you can stand on again and again without it cracking under pressure. It compounds. It sticks. It turns "**I had a good week**" into "this is just who I am now."

And the process is simple—not easy, simple. ***Name it. Explain it. Demonstrate it.*** Practice it. That's how anything solid gets built in your mind, body, and spirit. If you can say the habit out loud, tell yourself why it matters, show what it looks like in real life, and then reps-on-reps until it's automatic—you've got mastery. Once you've got mastery, there's no excuse not to apply it everywhere that counts.

Think about school. An all-nighter might save your grade once. Cool party trick. But it won't carry you through a degree, a career, or a life. What carries you is one focused hour a day. Brick by brick. Bricks become walls. Walls become a fortress. Suddenly you're not scrambling—you're operating from a foundation.

That's the trade: quick fixes for durable systems. Not vibes—rhythms. Goals you can measure and repeat. Fifty bucks into savings every payday. Three workouts a week whether you feel like it or not. Ten pages before you touch your phone. You don't jump ladders; you climb them. Rung by rung until "**wow**" sneaks up on you.

This is the heartbeat of **the Circle of Growth**. No hype. Just a loop you can actually run: identify what needs work, take a clean action, measure what happened, adjust the plan, and go again. Each cycle upgrades your baseline. Each pass removes friction. Before long, your calendar tells the story your character's been trying to write.

Scalable growth is the engine under the hood. Build it right and it won't just carry you through your 20s; it'll carry you through promotions, pivots, kids, crises, and whatever the economy decides to do next. Flashy fades. Rhythm lasts. Run the loop—then run it again.

Avoiding the "iPerson" Trap

Growth doesn't just test your habits—it tests your people skills. Not everyone you meet is good for your future. One of the biggest threats is the **iPerson**: all "**I, I, I,**" powered by ego, wrapped in low-grade negativity. You'll spot them fast. Ask a real question and they won't answer it—they'll dodge, perform, or pick a fight. You're seeking truth; they're protecting image.

Here's the difference. If you ask, "**What's one plus one?**" a growth-minded person might say "**Two,**" or even "**I'm not sure.**" Either way, the door is open. You can correct them, they learn, and both of you walk away better. Ask an **iPerson**, and you get noise—deflection, blame, conspiracy, everything but an actual answer. When ego runs the show, learning can't get in. No reflection, no adjustment, no growth. Flatline.

That's why **the Circle of Growth** starts with humility. It's not self-dragging; it's self-ownership. You look in the mirror and say, "**Here's where I missed. Here's what I'll do next.**" That moment isn't weakness—it's power. Responsibility gives you levers to pull. Victimhood leaves you waiting on the weather.

And don't get it twisted—using "**I**" isn't the problem. Ownership-I says, "**I messed up. I'm fixing it.**" Ego-I says, "**I'm never wrong,**" and burns a whole day defending the brand of Me. One builds momentum. The other builds walls. Pride keeps **iPeople** stuck in place while the rest of us lap the track.

So, protect your headspace. Keep your circle honest. If a conversation consistently turns into chaos, step back. You don't need to win the argument; you need to win your life. Real growth is simple math: reflection → adjustment → progress. The **iPerson** never gets past the first step. You will. Keep moving.

How You See the World

Visionary or Implementer

As you move through **the Circle of Growth**, you'll notice a pattern: how you see the world decides how you lead in it. Most of us tilt one way or the other—*Visionary* or *Implementer*. No heroes, no villains. Just different engines.

The Visionary lives in the "**not-yet,**" fueled by possibility and big swings. They're the friend who says, "**What if we built it bigger... and on Mars?**" The danger is drift—running so fast on ideas that nothing ever lands.

The Implementer lives in the "**right-now,**" fueled by structure, checklists, and receipts. They're the person who quietly turns chaos into a calendar. The danger is tunnel vision—getting so deep in the "**how**" that you forget the "**why.**"

Think architect and builder. One draws the future in lines; the other pours it in concrete. Take either one away and you're left with a fantasy or a file cabinet. **The Circle of Growth** doesn't pick sides—it makes the handshake happen. If you're heavy on vision, it teaches you to slow down just enough to translate dreams into steps: dates, owners, budgets, definitions of done. If you're strong on implementation, it pulls your head up so you can see the horizon, take smart risks, and choose projects that actually deserve your discipline.

Here's where it gets real. A Visionary without a system wakes up to ten "**genius**" ideas and no outcomes. The fix isn't killing the ideas; it's giving them a runway—one priority, one experiment, one metric. An Implementer without imagination crushes today's to-do list and accidentally builds a ladder against the wrong wall.

The fix isn't ditching discipline; it's scheduling curiosity—an hour a week to explore, to ask **"What would this look like if it were 10x better?"**

Once you can name your bias, you can train the opposite muscle. Explain how you naturally operate. Demonstrate a small move in the other lane. Practice it until it sticks. Visionaries practice cadence: fewer projects, clearer scopes, tighter feedback loops. Implementers practice altitude: bolder goals, wider context, room for iteration. That's scalable growth—stretching just far enough that next month's you is stronger than this month's, without snapping the system.

Complete leaders aren't born; they're built—loop by loop. **The Circle of Growth** gives you the rhythm to balance spark with structure, risk with reliability, **"why"** with **"how."** Keep your edge, grow your opposite, and watch your results stop looking random and start looking inevitable.

Part II

The Growth Grid

Interlude: The Journey II — Proof Before Spotlight

Yeshua wakes to the smell of coffee and the murmur of morning TV from the living room. The duplex feels different today—lighter, as if a window has been cracked open somewhere he can't see. He pads into the kitchen to find his mother, Lucía, at the table in her scrubs, hair pulled into a quick bun, nursing a chipped mug.

"You're up early for a day off," she says, eyes narrowing in that half-concerned, half-amused way only mothers possess.

"I went to see Eliza off," he says, pulling a glass from the cabinet. "And, uh... I did something else."

Her eyebrow rises a fraction. "Something good or something I'll need to call the pastor about?"

He laughs. "Good. I gave Frank my two weeks."

Silence. It's brief, but it lands. Lucía sets the mug down carefully, as if even the ceramic needs a second to absorb this. "You... you quit?" Her tone is neutral, a nurse's instinct to assess before reacting.

"I did." He meets her eyes, steady. "It's time."

A muscle in her jaw tightens and releases. Then she nods once, the smallest of approvals. "I wondered when you'd say that." She reaches across the table and squeezes his hand. "Just because something is good, m'ijo, doesn't mean it's still right. **When the** room gets too small, it's not rebellion to find the door. It's wisdom."

He exhales, tension he didn't know he carried easing from his shoulders. "I was worried you'd be scared for me."

"I'm your mother," she says, smiling softly. "I *am* scared. But fear is not a prison. **Name the risk, honor it, then act anyway.**" She gestures at the TV remote. "What's the plan?"

"Coach Barnes at the community college," he says. "A design apprenticeship—long shot, but I emailed. And… I think I need to build a real routine. Not just ideas—habits."

Lucía leans back, studying him the way she studies EKGs. "Then treat your day like a shift," she says. "Clock in to your future on purpose. **Schedule your courage; don't wait for it.**"

He grins. "Will you write all my pep talks?"

"Only if you cook dinner," she says, shooing him toward the door. "Go. Before you overthink and talk yourself out of it."

On the way out, he catches his reflection in the hallway mirror. Same face, same tired eyes—but behind them, a small flame has found oxygen.

Coach Barnes lives in a cramped office that smells of old leather and floor polish, walls lined with framed photos of teams long graduated. The man himself—early fifties, broad shoulders softening with age—holds court behind a desk that looks like it's witnessed at least five budget wars and three miracles.

"Well I'll be," Barnes says, leaning back with a grin when Yeshua steps in. "I heard whispers from Rosie's that the Mateo kid grew wings."

"That's a dramatic way to say I gave notice," Yeshua says, amused despite himself.

"Wings is what you need if you want out of Briarcliff gravity," Barnes replies. He gestures to a chair. "Sit. Let's inventory your assets: skills, time, cash, energy." He rattles the list off like a pre-game speech. "And your why. No student of mine gets out of here without a why tight as a spiral."

"Design," Yeshua says. "I like solving problems you can see. Signs, layouts, products—ways to make things clearer. But I'm ready to take any foothold that teaches me real work."

Barnes nods slowly. "We've got a tiny makerspace on campus. Laser cutter, 3D printer that mostly prints spaghetti, and a bulletin board that actually works." He smiles. "Nova Kim runs the place—a wizard with a soldering iron and a grant proposal. She's twenty-one, scrappy as a stray kitten. I'll ping her."

He types with two fingers, focus comically intense. A second later, his office door swings open and a young woman in a denim jacket and black beanie leans on the frame like she materialized from the hallway.

"You rang?" she says.

"Speak of the wizard," Barnes deadpans. "Nova, this is Yeshua. Yeshua, Nova. He's sober about work and allergic to shortcuts. He needs a small mountain to climb."

Nova sizes him up with bright, curious eyes. "You look like someone who's read instructions *and* ignored them."

"Both can be true," Yeshua says.

"Good," she says. "Come to the makerspace after lunch. We've got a farmers' market begging for better signage. If you can ship a prototype by Saturday, the stall owners will hug you or underpay you. Possibly both."

Barnes smirks. "He's also considering design apprenticeships and a few classes here. I want him to practice *on* something while those wheels turn."

"Practice is my love language," Nova replies. She tosses a keycard on Barnes's desk. "Use mine until they issue you one. But return it. I like my power."

She vanishes down the hall as efficiently as she appeared.

Barnes tilts his head at Yeshua. "She's a storm. Stay close enough to learn, far enough not to get electrocuted."

"I can manage," Yeshua says, heart thudding with the thrill of a real project. **You don't find confidence; you build it by shipping.** He stands to leave, then pauses. "Coach—thanks."

"Son," Barnes says, eyes briefly soft, "talent is common. Follow-through is rare. **Make your word heavier than your mood.** That's how you'll win."

The campus makerspace is a narrow room tucked between a storage closet and a stairwell, patched together like a treehouse built by ambitious teenagers. Pegboards offer up tools like candy.

A half-assembled drone sleeps on a table, and two students argue amiably about whether their filament jam is artistic.

Nova waves him toward a whiteboard scrawled with ideas: Market Map, Legibility Tests, Weather Durability, Vendor Voices.

"We gather first, we guess second," she says, eyes sparkling. "You know the stalls?"

"Seen them. Signs are… bad," he says politely.

"Brutal is the word," Nova says. "Cursive fonts so curly you could tie a boat to them. Colors that fight each other like cousins at a wedding." She throws a stack of polaroids on the table. "We interviewed five vendors. They want three things: carts found faster, products understood fast, prices visible. Read these and sketch."

He reads. Strawberries mislabeled as "Summer Jewels." A jam stall whose price list lives on a damp napkin. A local woodworker whose gorgeous pieces hide behind a camouflage of competing signs.

"Make me three prototypes by four o'clock," Nova says, tapping the table thrice. "One minimal, one bold, one friendly. We'll field-test them Friday. Real humans, real eyes, real sun." She pauses. "Design lives and dies in the wild. **Test your ideas where they have to survive.**"

He loses himself in the work, pencils scratching, measurements scribbled, mind buzzing. He hadn't realized how hungry he was for this—problems you can touch, feedback that arrives in the tilt of a buyer's head. Nova roams the room like a benevolent warden, occasionally swooping in to ask, "Why this font?" or "What does this color make you *feel* if you hadn't slept?"

By three-fifty, he has three poster boards—clean, legible, humble. Nova assesses them with the seriousness of a judge unbribed by cupcakes. "This one," she says, tapping the minimal design. "You made the strawberries look like a decision, not a rumor." She grins. "Friday, you and I are running a tiny experiment."

"What about the vendors?" he asks.

"We got permission," she says. "We just show up before the market opens, swap signs on one stall, and watch. Count the pauses. Count the questions. Count the sales if they let us. **Measure the change you want to believe in.**"

"Who else is helping?" he asks.

Nova winks. "I recruit interesting people like a crow collects shiny things. Speaking of which, come with me."

She herds him down a back staircase to a small auto bay tucked behind a vocational classroom. A young man in coveralls, forearms grease-streaked, hums along to a playlist while adjusting the hinge on a door panel. He looks up as they approach: sharp eyes, dimpled grin, posture that says *I take care of the things I touch.*

"Kyrie Alvarez," Nova announces. "Mechanic. Former state runner-up, small forward and big heart. He runs Alvarez Auto on Maple. He keeps my scooter alive out of sheer pity."

Kyrie wipes his hands and offers one. His handshake is warm and straightforward. "Nova told me you shipped something today."

"A prototype," Yeshua says. "Shipping tomorrow."

"Same thing," Kyrie replies. "You showed up. She says you might need a tune-up." He gestures at a whiteboard with columns: Problem → Root Cause → Next Experiment → Lesson. Today's line reads: "Door squeak—dust + dry hinges—clean + lube—'Squeak gone but latch stiff; adjust torque.'"

Yeshua points, impressed. "You run experiments in a body shop?"

Kyrie laughs. "What did you think we did? Vibe the cars into compliance?" He grins. "I got tired of feeling like every day was a rerun. So I built a board like this to force myself to learn out loud. **Improve the process and the product improves itself.**"

Nova elbows Kyrie lightly. "He's humble when he's not scoring on you in pickup games," she says.

"Facts," Kyrie says. He glances at Yeshua, reading more than his expression. "You look like someone who just walked off a map."

"I quit my job," Yeshua says. "Two weeks from free fall."

Kyrie nods once, as if this fits into a pattern he already respects. "Then your job now is tiny wins. Not big speeches. **Stack small proof until your mind believes you.**" He tosses Yeshua a rag. "Wipe your hands. You're gonna be touching a lot of new tools."

They talk gear and routines until Nova's watch chirps. "Budget meeting," she says, grimacing. "Come by Alvarez Auto Saturday. I'll bring coffee. Kyrie, bring your borderline questionable advice."

"It's legally actionable," Kyrie says solemnly. "See you, man."

The following morning, the farmers' market yawns awake under a soft sun. Vendors assemble their booths with the reverence of stagehands before opening night. The air smells like herbs and cut wood. Nova and Yeshua arrive early, swap in the new sign on Mrs. Ramirez's strawberry stall with her blessing, and step back to watch.

It's a surprisingly tense thrill, waiting to see whether a few lines and letters can change the shape of a morning. They watch two shoppers beeline to the strawberries, pause, pick up cartons. Another customer, who'd drifted by the old sign yesterday, stops at the new one, eyes widening. "Strawberries, two for five? Oh, that's clear. I'll take two." Mrs. Ramirez glances at them with a what-are-you-two-up-to smile.

"Count?" Nova murmurs.

"Three intentional pauses, two baskets purchased so far," Yeshua says, scribbling on a pad. He feels ridiculous and alive. "Clarity tax paid back."

They run the quick test for an hour, track an uptick that's not huge but noticeable. Mrs. Ramirez insists they take a carton for free. Nova declines, then buys two in solidarity. "Work should taste like something," she says, juice on her fingers. "This tastes like *evidence*."

They're packing up when a glossy poster catches Yeshua's eye, taped to the old brick wall by the community board—a black-and-silver announcement with a sharp serif font: **MALIK DRAVEN — ONE NIGHT ONLY — BUILD THE BRAND THAT BUILDS YOUR LIFE**. The photo shows a man in his late twenties, suit cut razor precise, gaze direct enough to feel personal. The tagline at the bottom: *Stop being invisible. Be the room.*

Nova follows his gaze and makes a face. "Careful. That man sells gravity to planets."

"You know him?" Yeshua asks.

"By reputation," she says. "He runs a 'leadership accelerator.' Big on 'perception is reality.' Slick events, slicker invoices. Some folks swear by him. Some swear at him."

"Is it a scam?" Yeshua asks.

"Scam is a strong word," Nova says carefully. "He's a specialist. **He teaches spotlight. But if you haven't built a stage, the light can blind you.**"

The poster boasts an event at the high school auditorium next Friday. Free entry, limited VIP meet-and-greet. Yeshua feels the tug, the *what if*. An easy solution to being stuck. A promise with better lighting. He files the feeling away, cautious and curious.

As they step from shade back into sun, a familiar voice calls Yeshua's name. He turns to find a young woman at a folding table strewn with neatly labeled recipe cards and a money tin that probably reconciles to the cent. She has kind eyes behind round glasses and an apron that reads "Bean There."

"Priya," Nova says, delighted. "Yeshua, meet Priya Sharma. She runs the thrift pop-up on Tuesdays and keeps this market solvent."

"I keep the *books*," Priya corrects, smiling. "Solvency is a team sport." She gestures at the poster in his hand. "You thinking of going to that?"

"Curious," he admits.

"Curiosity is good," she says. "I went last year. He's charismatic, convincing, and almost right about everything." She pauses, choosing her words. "Just remember: **There's a difference between building a *brand* and building a *business*.** One pays you in applause, the other in invoices."

Nova claps lightly. "Put that on a billboard."

Priya's gaze lingers on Yeshua's notepad, his careful tallies. "You taking notes at a farmers' market?"

"Testing a sign," he says, a little embarrassed. "Trying to get serious."

Priya's smile warms. "Serious is cheap. Systems are expensive," she says. "If you want help budgeting your time and money while you jump, I can show you my spreadsheet. It has colors."

"Beware," Nova stage-whispers. "Her cells have rules. They obey her."

"I like rules," Yeshua says, surprising himself. "At least the ones I make."

"Good answer," Priya says. "Monday night at the library? I'll bring the template. You bring your numbers. **Buy back time on paper before you spend it in the wild.**"

As they walk away, Nova bumps his shoulder. "You collect good people quick," she says. "It's a skill."

"I watched you do it first," he says. "Crows teach crows."

"Careful," she says, grinning. "Next I'll teach you to steal shiny budget surpluses."

Monday night, the library's study room hums with fluorescent light and the soft percussion of keys. Priya's laptop glows with an immaculate spreadsheet. Each tab is a universe: Rent, Food, Gas, Subscriptions, "Fun (Modest)," and a tab titled "Runway" that makes Yeshua sit up straighter.

"Your two-week notice starts a clock," Priya says, fingers flying. "We plan backwards from it." She inputs his income, savings (meager), likely side work (possible), and fixed expenses (stubborn). "Okay. If we tighten here and here," she highlights, "we can get you a three-month runway. That's the difference between panic and progress."

Yeshua watches the numbers form patterns under her hands. He's never seen his life this tidy. He feels exposed and relieved. "I didn't know 'Fun (Modest)' was a line item."

"It better be," Priya says. "Burnout is expensive. **If it's not on the calendar and the budget, it's a fantasy.**"

He nods, a wry smile tugging. "You're right. I've had a lot of fantasies."

"Then let's upgrade them to plans." She turns the laptop to him. "Set two auto transfers: one to savings, one to 'Education/Tools.' Fifty dollars each per paycheck, starting now. Small numbers, big signal."

"Signal?"

"You're telling Future You: 'We take ourselves seriously now.'" She leans back, studying him. "That look on your face—what's the story?"

"Story?"

"What you're telling yourself," she says, gentle but insistent. "Is it 'I'm behind'? 'I'm late'? 'I'll be found out'?"

He hesitates. "Maybe all three."

"Rewrite it," she says simply. "**Say the true thing you can live with, not the loud lie you can't.** Try: 'I'm early to my own life.'"

He lets the sentence sit in his mouth like a new spice. It tastes strange and good.

Saturday at Alvarez Auto, Kyrie moves through the bay with a dancer's economy. A Kaizen board—simple, clear—hangs where everyone can see it. A younger tech, Tino, finishes an oil change and pins a card to "Lessons." Kyrie fist bumps him. "Teach the next shift," he says. "Knowledge lost is money lost."

Yeshua lingers near the board, reading. He likes that nothing pretends. The shop admits problems and records fixes with unembarrassed honesty. **Truth first. Ego later.** He recognizes the relief of working in a room where the scoreboard is public.

"Grab that torque wrench," Kyrie calls. "Feel the difference between snug and safe."

They work in companionable rhythm, conversation meandering across music, high school coaches, why some people chase speedboats and others chase sleep. Kyrie listens with his eyes, a present kind of attention.

"You going to that Draven thing?" Kyrie asks eventually, casual.

"Maybe," Yeshua says. "I want to hear what he says about getting noticed."

"'Getting noticed' is a magnet," Kyrie says, tightening a bolt with care. "Pulls in nails and bottle caps. Sharp and shiny, both. **If you can't sort what you attract, attention becomes wreckage.**" He shrugs. "But go. Hear him. Just don't outsource your spine."

Nova arrives with coffee and a smug apology for being "creatively late." She hands Yeshua a cup marked with a tiny lightning bolt doodle. "For your experiments," she says. "Caffeine is a control variable."

Priya shows up an hour later with a plastic folder labeled "Templates" and the unbothered energy of someone who knows their receipts by heart. She watches Yeshua help Tino re-mount a tire and nods. "Shoulders relaxed. That's a good sign," she says. "People who trust themselves don't white-knuckle wrenches."

It dawns on Yeshua that he's accidentally built a little crew—each one a teacher in a different dialect of the same language: competence without theatrics. He doesn't name that blessing aloud. He doesn't want to spook it.

The Friday of Malik Draven's event arrives with the ache of weather about to change. Posters have multiplied like mushrooms after rain—barbershop, bakery, the bulletin board at the co-op. The high school auditorium, unused since spring, hums back to life under stage lights rented for the occasion.

Yeshua takes a seat near the middle, Nova on his left, Priya on his right, Kyrie a row behind with Tino, arms folded like a skeptic forced to attend church. The crowd is young and eager, with a scattering of older faces curious about new medicine. The energy has the same electric expectancy of homecoming games—something about to happen, all eyes forward.

At eight sharp, the house lights dim and the stage lights flare. The man himself steps into the spotlight: Malik Draven. He's as the poster promised—razor suit, controlled smile, gaze that moves like a scanner. He stands with the posture of a man measuring rooms for mirrors.

"Good evening, Briarcliff," he says, voice warm, calibrated. "I came because small towns hold big dreams. I came because somebody here is ready to be seen."

Applause rolls like a wave. Yeshua claps politely, watchful.

Malik's talk is good. Infuriatingly good. He's funny, self-deprecating when it serves him, sharp when he wants you to feel the edge of your own excuses. He tells a story about getting laughed out of a pitch meeting at twenty-one, then being invited back at twenty-four to sell the product to the same people who mocked him. He says he learned that day that the room didn't change—*he* did.

"You don't need permission," Malik says, prowling the stage. "You need presence. You need a message so clean it cuts, and the courage to repeat it until the room remembers your name. **Rehearse who you are until reality has to catch up.**"

The crowd drinks it in. Nova scribbles in a tiny notebook, eyebrows knit. Priya watches, still. Kyrie leans forward, expression unreadable.

Then Malik steps closer to the line that had your friends cautioning you.

"People think they need to build products before they build perception," he says, smile widening. "That's slow. That's old. Attention is the accelerant. **Be the person they can't ignore, then build the thing they can't live without.**"

Applause spikes. Yeshua feels the pull, hot and sweet. He also feels something else—a splinter under the fingernail of his attention.

Nova leans over and whispers, "That line cuts both ways."

Priya adds, even softer, "Be careful whose applause you're working for."

The Q&A is expertly managed. Malik calls on a shy teenager and folds her dream into a soundbite. He compliments a barber's logo then suggests a small change that will "triple retention," and the room laughs like they've been let into a secret. He has presence—no sense denying what your bones know.

At the end, Malik offers a VIP meet-and-greet—"fifteen minutes that could change your next fifteen months." The line forms fast, all bright eyes and vibrating phones. Yeshua's feet carry him down the aisle before his brain can finish a debate. His friends don't stop him. They don't cheer either. They let him walk into the light to see if it warms or burns.

Malik's assistant, a woman with a tablet and the clipped efficiency of someone who eats calendars, scans the line. "Name?" she asks, tone practiced.

"Yeshua Mateo," he says, feeling suddenly provincial.

"Lovely," she says, eyes flicking over him. "First time seeing Malik?"

He nods.

"Tell him a sentence he can work with," she advises, surprisingly kind. "**Long stories die in short rooms.**"

By the time Yeshua reaches the front, Malik is still crisp, still focused—no degradation in wattage. That alone earns respect. Malik extends a hand. His grip is firm, temperature neutral.

"Yeshua," he says, reading the card the assistant slid him. "You have a memorable name. What are you building?"

"I'm... redesigning signs for our farmers' market," he says, hating how small it sounds and hating himself for hating it. "Learning design by shipping. I quit my diner job to pursue more."

Malik's smile doesn't change. "Good. You chose motion over memory." His eyes sharpen. "Now say a cleaner sentence."

Yeshua inhales. "I make local businesses easier to find and buy from," he says. The sentence surprises him as much as anyone.

"Better," Malik says. He glances at the assistant. "Note: clarity under pressure." Then back to Yeshua. "You'll need two things next: audience and offer. Momentum demands both. **Without audience, you push alone. Without offer, you pull air.** Start a weekly post highlighting one vendor you improve. Before/after photos. Three lines max. Tag them. Make your work visible."

"That feels like bragging," Yeshua says before he can catch the insecurity.

"Visibility is not vanity," Malik says smoothly. "It's oxygen. Just beware the mirror becoming a mask."

The phrase lands like an omen. **Beware the mirror becoming a mask.** Yeshua files it under things to parse later.

Malik presses a glossy card into his palm. "We run a cohort next month. Expensive. Worth it if you're ready. If not, come back when you have case studies. Either way, decide. **Indecision is just fear in a tuxedo.**"

The assistant is already moving the line. Yeshua steps aside, head buzzing. He feels both seen and sold to. It's a disorienting cocktail.

He rejoins his friends in the lobby, where the overhead lights remind him he's back on earth. Nova watches his face like a seismograph.

"Well?" she asks.

"He's good," Yeshua says. "He told me to make my work visible. Weekly posts, before/afters."

"That's… not bad advice," Priya admits. "For free."

"Yeah," Kyrie says slowly. "The dangerous bit is when the post becomes the project. **Proof beats performance.**"

"I'll make sure the work stays the work," Yeshua says.

"Then do it," Nova replies. "Three posts. Three weeks. We'll check if it moves anything real."

"Deal," he says. He glances at Malik's card in his hand—thick stock, embossed logo, a phone number that probably answers. He slips it into his wallet and feels its weight.

That night, back in his room, he doesn't reach for the shoebox. He opens a blank document and writes:

Week 1: Clarity Test — Mrs. Ramirez Strawberries

- Before: Cursive sign, low legibility, price unclear.

- After: Bold, high-contrast, price visible.

- Result: +12 pauses in 60 minutes; 2 additional baskets purchased; one returning customer said, "I didn't see you last time—this helps."

Week 2: The Jam List (planned)

Week 3: The Woodworker's Window (planned)

He drafts a short post that is not a sermon. It's a record. He resists the urge to add cleverness. He adds a simple photo: before on the left, after on the right. He sets a Sunday morning schedule reminder.

He also creates a folder called "Case Studies," because it makes him feel like a person with files and not just feelings.

Before bed, a text lights his phone.

ELIZA: *Am I allowed to be proud yet or do I have to wait for permission?*

YESHUA: *Permission granted. Also, started a project. And met a man selling spotlights.*

ELIZA: *Don't look directly at it. Also, send pics. Of the signs, not the man.*

He laughs in the dark. The tension eases.

As he's about to set the phone down, another notification: an email reply from the design apprenticeship contact, subject line: "Re: Late inquiry."

He swallows, opens it.

Yeshua—thanks for reaching out. We're full this cycle, but your initiative is noted. If you can send two small case studies by the end of the month, we'll consider you for a rolling spot.

He reads it twice to be sure. His heart kicks. Not a yes, not a no. A door propped open by work.

He closes his eyes and whispers a thank you to no one in particular. **Opportunity respects the prepared, not the perfect.** He writes a sticky note and slaps it on the wall above his desk: "Two case studies—by the 30th." He smiles. That's not a dream. That's a deadline.

As he slides under the covers, he lets the day replay: Nova's quick mind, Kyrie's steady hands, Priya's fierce spreadsheets, Malik's clean sentences that cut both ways. He sees himself walking two lines—the quiet line of competence and the bright line of attention—and he knows which one must lead.

Tomorrow, he'll meet the woodworker and ask permission to rebuild the sign. He'll wear sunscreen and carry water and bring extra zip ties because something always needs tying. He'll count pauses and questions and sales if they'll trust him with the numbers. He'll post on Sunday. He'll write Coach Barnes with an update and ask which classes fill fastest. He'll drink coffee too late and regret it and do it again.

The loop is small: act → observe → learn → adjust. It's almost boring. He smiles in the dark. Boring is the point. Boring, done enough times, becomes magic.

On his nightstand, Malik's card glints under the streetlight seeping through the blinds. He flips it face-down and turns off the lamp.

The Growth Grid
How You're Wired to Grow

Let's get personal for a second: how do you like to grow? Not how your boss thinks you should grow. Not what your feed says is winning this week. You. Because drifting through roles that don't fit is how capable people end up exhausted and average. Motion isn't growth. Alignment is. When your path matches your design, progress stops feeling like punishment and starts feeling like purpose.

That's why I built the **Growth Grid**—a simple way to name your natural lane so you can stop forcing a life that doesn't fit and start building one that does.

Some of us are **Contributors** at heart: we breathe easier when there's order, rhythm, and a clean process. Give us a system and we'll make it sing, day after day. That's not small—it's the foundation everything else stands on. Your edge is consistency; your next level is deep systems thinking, so the machine runs smoother because you touched it.

Some of us are **Independent Creators**: freedom is fuel, and we want our effort tied directly to our outcome. We make, we ship, we learn, we repeat. Your edge is originality; your next level is channeling that energy into a craft and a business model that pays you for being you—not for playing office.

Some of us are **Visionary Builders**: we see the big picture and can get people moving toward it. We collect talent, raise the scaffolding, and turn **"what if"** into **"we did."** Your edge is scale; your next level is pairing vision with structure, so the dream doesn't collapse when it gets heavy.

And some of us are **Strategic Investors**: we think in decades, not days. We look for leverage, ownership, and assets that compound while we sleep. Your edge is patience; your next level is designing engines that create opportunity for others, not just returns for yourself.

None of these paths is "**better**." They're different kinds of power. The trap is pretending to be one you're not. If you're a Creator, that rigid corporate ladder will squeeze the life out of you. If you're a Builder, playing small will make you restless and resentful. If you're an Investor, short-term hustle will bore you to death. If you're a Contributor, chasing every shiny new thing will drown your gift in chaos.

When you know your grid, you know your growth. You pick work that fits your wiring. You set goals that match your engine. You build a week that feels like you—not a costume you wear from nine to five. That's the move from surviving to thriving. That's where **the Circle of Growth** hits different: it doesn't ask you to be everything; it trains you to be your thing on purpose—and then build the systems to make it sustainable.

Circle of Growth Mantra

"*I am growth in motion*.

I lead with **vision**, walk with **values**, and live on **mission**.

I face the **truth** within me, **not to judge** it—but to rise from it.

I choose **courage** over *comfort*, **clarity** over *chaos*, and **character** over *convenience*.

I **stand** in *humility*, **learn** with *intention*, and **execute** with *discipline*.

I am not here to chase *success*—I am here to *build it*, *shape it*, and *multiply it*.

Because leadership **starts with me**—but it never ends with me.

This is **the Circle of Growth**. And **I move in it with purpose**."

Part III

The Three Stages of Growth

Interlude

The Journey III — Trial by Clarity

The post goes live on Sunday at 8:00 a.m. The photograph—before on the left, after on the right—sits like a neat truth. The caption is small: *Clarity test at the Briarcliff Market. One hour, one new sign. 12 extra pauses. Two extra baskets. Design is a decision, not a decoration.* He presses "publish," then locks his phone in the kitchen drawer as a kindness to himself.

By nine, the drawer rattles—Eliza, Coach Barnes, two former regulars from Rosie's, and an email from a vendor he doesn't know: *Can you do mine next?*

He walks instead. Briarcliff on a Sunday has the washed, careful quiet of a pressed shirt. He passes the marquee outside the high school—**MALIK DRAVEN—SOLD OUT** still clings to the letters—and turns toward Maple, where the woodworker he's been meaning to meet keeps a narrow shop with a bell that's an optimist.

The bell rings twice before anyone appears. The man who steps from the back wears a canvas apron and the expression of someone who is unfinished with three thoughts at once.

"Hale," he says, sticking out a hand. "If you're selling magazines or salvation, I've got both already."

"Yeshua," he answers. "I'm selling legibility."

Hale grunts in a way that might be interest. His showroom is a portrait of reticence: beautiful things half-hidden behind price tags that look like apologies. "People come in and say 'how lovely' and leave," Hale says matter-of-factly. "Lovely doesn't pay the light bill."

Yeshua takes in the clues: a stool at the exact place the floorboards are scuffed, a kettle just off-boil, a ledger open to a day with too many zeros. He opens his notebook.

"I'd like to prototype a sign for your window," he says. "Not the whole story—just the first sentence. Chairs in the window, prices big enough to read from across the street, one line about the wood."

Hale watches him the way a cat watches a clock. "What do you get out of this?"

"Practice. A case study. If it works, you can pay me with money. If it doesn't, you can pay me with a hard truth."

Hale considers, then nods once. "Put 'White Oak' in the sentence. If a thing has a name, it stands up straighter."

Yeshua sketches. He keeps the colors strict—ink black on white—and lets the wood speak for itself. When he finishes, Hale inclines his head the way a man tips his hat to a good argument.

"You come back Tuesday," Hale says. "We'll put your sentence in my window."

Make the first sentence do more than greet; make it *guide*.

At the library that evening, Priya has claimed a table under the stern portrait of a founder who looks offended by decimals. She is not offended. She has created a new tab called "Weather" and filled it with contingencies.

"Forecast says Friday may drown," she says, tapping the screen. "Your strawberry science works in the sun. What do you do if the sky heckles?"

"Test indoors," he says. "Marjorie's Jams. The church fellowship hall. Any place with foot traffic and fluorescent lights."

Priya nods, pleased at the lack of poetry. "And a materials budget?" She slides him a neat list. "Plastic sleeves. Painter's tape. A rain-safe marker that won't smudge when a child weaponizes a juice box."

He winces, appreciating the specificity. "I can cover this."

"Covering is one thing," she says. "Planning is better. **Buy resilience before you have to rent it at panic prices.**"

She glances over his shoulder. "Zee," she calls softly. "You're early."

A figure lingers at the doorway—camera bag crossbody, hair bleached the precise shade of a noonday cloud. They enter as if asking permission from the light.

"This is Zadie Moreno," Priya says. "Zee to friends and to anyone who spells Zadie wrong. Film student, A/V desk wizard, and very gentle with microphones."

Zee offers a shy, practiced half-smile. "Priya said you're doing before-and-afters," they say. "If you want them to travel, let them move." They pat the camera. "Motion reads as proof. Still photos read as marketing."

"I don't want marketing," Yeshua says, surprising himself with the firmness of it. "I want a record."

Zee's eyes warm, the way light does when it rests on a page. "Then I'll shoot like a court reporter," they say. "Simple coverage. No fiddly transitions. **Evidence first; aesthetics second.**"

Nova arrives ten minutes late with a tote bag and a breathless apology that smells faintly of solder. She looks Zee over like a museum curator acquiring a favorite piece. "You film like you built a tripod out of principles," she says. "Good."

Kyrie texts he'll be late: *Customer's check engine light is a candle of confusion. Don't wait.*

They don't. They put the week in a grid. Monday—Hale's window. Tuesday—Marjorie's price board. Wednesday—Post-production and Priya's checks. Thursday—Bottleneck removal (Nova's phrase). Friday—Farmers' market (weather permitting). Sunday—Post.

They keep the lines short. They draw a circle in the margin: **Identify → Act → Measure → Adjust**. Nova taps it twice.

"Loop," she says. "Everything lives or dies by the loop."

On Tuesday, the weather decides to demonstrate contempt for optimism. Rain needles the sidewalks; puddles behave like small, organized conspiracies. Marjorie's fellowship hall smells of coffee, wax, and the long memory of casseroles. The jam stall today is a fold-out table and a woman with forearms that can lift a pot without a grunt.

"Prices on napkins," Marjorie says, wry. "At my age, that's a crime against sight."

They pin the new board behind the table: three columns—flavor, ingredients, price—and a short line at the top: *Local fruit. Low sugar. Honest jars.* It looks spare in a room that loves clutter.

They test for an hour. The data arrives in nods and quick decisions. An old man in a windbreaker says "thank you" to a board as if it can hear. A child reads "Strawberry-Rhubarb" aloud like it's a spell.

Zee films with the precision of someone who has opinions about frames per second. They keep the lens plain and the angle honest. When Nova tries to rearrange a pyramid of jars for "visual interest," Zee murmurs, "We're reporters today," and Nova lifts her hands in surrender.

They tally: seven new purchases, four questions answered by the board before the mouth could form them. Marjorie counts her bills, then looks at Yeshua as if deciding whether he's a phase or a tool.

"You may put your name under the board," she says. "In small letters. If I can read it without my readers, it's too big."

Yeshua prints "Sign by Mateo" so small it feels like a secret handshake. He resists the impulse to photograph that line. He photographs the jars instead.

If the work is true, it will point back to you without you pointing at yourself.

The email from Malik's assistant arrives mid-afternoon, subtle as a hand at the small of the back.

Yeshua—Malik enjoyed your question and your sentence. We're curating a "Spotlight Hour" on Thursday—three local builders, ten minutes each, a livestream. No fee, no pitch. Just visibility. Interested?

Nova reads over his shoulder without apology. "He names the bait 'no pitch' so you'll think it's not bait," she says. "But it's... not not an opportunity."

Priya steeples her fingers. "Ten minutes to show the loop in public could be useful," she admits. "**If you show the loop and not the legend.**"

Kyrie, arriving in a drift of clean rain with a clean shirt, shrugs. "Do it if you can stand up straight after," he says. "Some stages bend your posture."

"What if I set a rule?" Yeshua says. "No 'I' unless it's about the process. No future tense. Only what we've measured."

Nova snorts. "You're going to bring a ruler to theater."

"Good," Priya says. "Most people bring glitter."

He texts back: *Yes, if I can show two case studies and talk process only.* The assistant replies quickly: *Refreshing. See you Thursday. Send assets by Wednesday at noon.*

Assets. He looks at Zee.

"I'll cut clean," Zee says. "Titles like a newspaper. No adjectives that aren't numbers."

They agree on three on-screen lines: *Before/After. Time window. Result.* He feels steadier. The mirror is present; he will not let it become a mask.

Avoid the iPerson Trap: don't turn your identity into your instrument. Build the instrument; let identity be the quiet echo.

Hale's window takes three tries to get right. The first version is too clever. The second is shy. The third begins like a sentence a busy person can finish with a purchase: *White Oak Chairs — Built to Outlast the Arguments They'll Hear.* The price sits, unembarrassed, to the right.

Hale reads it aloud and huffs—something like approval disguised as complaint. "You made me sound like a man with a plan," he says.

"You made you sound like that," Yeshua says. "I just put it where strangers can hear."

They clean the window, tape the letters with the kind of attention small towns reserve for weddings and weather. Zee films from across the street as the first passerby stops dead, reads, steps inside.

"Count," Nova whispers, even though no one is in danger of forgetting.

By noon, three chairs go out the door. Hale's ledger receives numbers as if grateful for company. He writes an invoice for Yeshua by hand and tears it off with a neat sound.

"Take this," he says, pressing it into Yeshua's palm. "So you remember you aren't playing."

Yeshua looks down at the number, more than he expected. "This is generous."

"This is math," Hale says. "You and your sentence put iron in my day. Iron isn't free."

Take money without flinching when it's tied to value you actually created.

Across the street, a new poster has sprouted, unrolled during lunch like a flag: **DRAVEN BRAND LAB—COHORT APPLICATIONS OPEN.** The paper smells expensive in the rain. Many things smell expensive in the rain.

Kyrie eyes it with the mild, even disdain he keeps for tools that don't fit his hand. "He's quick," he says. "He salts the ground where a crop is about to come up."

"Or he's just running his playbook on schedule," Priya says. "Correlation isn't conspiracy."

"Both can be true," Nova says. "Truth often arrives in pairs and asks you to choose your discomfort."

Thursday's "Spotlight Hour" is in the auditorium lobby—a half-circle of lights, a dove-gray backdrop, chairs pitched at an angle that flatters jawlines. A small audience forms; the rest will watch on phones. Malik makes his entrance with no fanfare this time—only a nod to the camera, oddly respectful of the lens's authority.

Yeshua's segment is second. He chooses a tone pitched between field report and shop talk. He shows strawberries, then jars, then chairs. He names numbers and durations. He names his crew—Nova, Priya, Kyrie, Zee—each with one sentence about why they matter. He does not say "brand." He says "process" until the word feels like a floor you can stand on.

Malik listens with that unblinking attention, the kind that makes some people confess and others perform better. When the ten minutes end, Malik doesn't add flare. He says, "You are building muscles that survive." It sounds like a benediction and a warning at once.

Afterward, in the edge-of-stage quiet, Malik approaches.

"Good," he says, the word as precise as a ruler. "You made silence do work. Keep that."

He studies Yeshua a second longer than comfort allows. "Be careful, Mateo," he says lightly, but not like a joke. "**The crowd will try to hire you to be the version of you that entertains them most.** Don't sign that contract."

Yeshua nods, thankful and wary at once.

As they leave, Nova taps the side of her nose. "He's not the villain I wanted," she admits. "He's the test I expected."

Kyrie folds a chair with the grace of a practiced stagehand. "Tests don't care if you like them," he says. "They care if you learned."

The next farmer's market opens under a weather truce—low clouds like undecided jurors. Hale lends two chairs to the woodworker's neighbor, who had complained that the new sign created a line "that wasn't there before, thanks," as if lines are zero-sum. Yeshua negotiates the space with tape and courtesy, then adds a small directional arrow that moves people in a gentle curve instead of a trample. The neighbor mutters a reluctant thanks that would evaporate if exposed to heat.

They run their counts; they don't argue with what arrives. Priya logs the hours in a sheet that is slowly beginning to look like a story without adjectives. Zee's video of "Before/After—Mrs. Ramirez" crosses a thousand views, which means precisely nothing and probably something; they decide to call it "context" and move on.

At noon, the sky delivers on its earlier threat. The rain isn't a tantrum; it is a policy. Vendors fold their tents with the practised competence of people who know timing. Nova keeps the signs up long enough to see if legibility survives under gray; it does. The tape gives up before the type does. She makes a note: **Next time, buy better tape.**

As they wrestle a flapping banner into compliance, a white SUV glides to the curb. The passenger window descends like a stage cue, and Malik—no jacket, white shirt rolled to the elbows—leans toward the opening.

"Need a hand?" he calls, voice just loud enough.

"No," Nova says cheerfully. "We need better tape."

"I can't help there," he says, smiling, "but I can offer shelter. There's coffee at the auditorium."

Yeshua thanks him. It is the right sentence. Malik nods, reads the rain the way he reads rooms, and raises the window. The SUV glides away; the banner, newly subdued, snaps once like a fish and then accepts its fate.

Kyrie watches the street long after the vehicle is gone. "He didn't have to stop," he says.

"No one ever has to stop," Priya says. "That's why it counts when they do."

"Or why it's useful," Nova says, practical. "Nothing wrong with useful, if you keep your soul."

When someone powerful offers a shortcut, check both where it starts and where it ends.

They debrief at Rosie's, the diner lights reflecting in the laminated menu like stars that can be ordered with fries. The four of them and Zee occupy a booth that has witnessed proposals, breakups, and the quiet decision to start again. Lucía slides a slice of pie onto the table without asking.

"You look like people who earned a pie," she says. "That's different from wanting one."

They map the week on napkins. What failed? Tape. What worked? Numbers beat narratives. What surprised? Hale smiling and not dying of it. What's next? The "Asset" tab in Priya's sheet gets a new line: *Tripod—owned* after Zee insists on paying half.

Yeshua listens more than he speaks. He notices things: that Nova's confidence is a muscle she keeps in pockets when not needed; that Priya's laughter is rare and therefore valuable; that Kyrie talks to problems as if they are employees who can be retrained; that Zee dislikes attention unless it is pointed at the work.

"You're quiet," Lucía says, topping up coffee for the table and violating three refills rules with impunity.

"Thinking," he says. "This week felt... adult."

"Adult is when you keep your appointments with yourself," she says. "The rest is shoes."

They laugh, because Lucía has a way of lifting the weight and leaving the lesson.

On the way out, Yeshua stops at the bulletin board by the door. The Draven poster has been replaced by a new announcement, same font, same silver: **MALIK DRAVEN—BRAND LAB SCHOLARSHIPS—APPLY IF YOU BUILD.** A QR code stares like an invitation and a dare.

Kyrie snorts. "He reads the market," he says. "He knows when to discount."

"Or when to invest," Priya says. "People use the same word to mean different things and wonder why they argue."

"Pick your meaning," Nova says. "Then pick your move."

They don't scan the code. Not tonight. They choose pancakes.

At midnight, in the quiet that applies balm to towns like a salve, an email arrives from the apprenticeship program.

Yeshua—your two case studies are clear, specific, and refreshing. We hold a trial day next Wednesday. Bring your tools, your notebook, and one question you don't know how to answer yet. We'll supply the chaos.

He leans back in his chair and stares at the ceiling, a crooked smile choosing his face. He had promised himself he would not chase better lighting. He would chase better loops. And here is a door, plain, unlit, patient.

He writes the question on a sticky note and presses it next to the others: *How do you scale clarity without scaling chaos?*

He doesn't expect an answer tonight. He expects work.

He turns Malik's card over in his wallet and writes a rule across the embossed logo in pencil before sliding it back: **Proof—then spotlight. Spiral up, not out.**

He sets his alarm for the morning wrap-up with Hale and the follow-up with Marjorie. He texts the crew—*Trial day Wednesday. We're in the game.* They answer in their dialects: Nova with a lightning bolt, Priya with a green check, Kyrie with a wrench, Zee with a camera emoji and a heart small enough to fit between numbers.

He switches off the lamp and, in the dark, rehearses a life that doesn't require rehearsal—routines that move on rails, friends that catch you if you lean too far into your own story, work that pays its own way. Somewhere down Main, a poster curls with the damp and falls, quietly, to the pavement.

Stages of Growth

The Comfort Zone — the first stage of growth, and the easiest place to get stuck.

It feels like home because it's familiar, predictable, soft around the edges. But comfort isn't a sanctuary—it's a slow, quiet cage. You don't notice the bars going up because they're made of moments: a teacher's throwaway comment, a report card that stung, a fall off a bike that turned into **"never again."** Brick by brick, the story becomes identity. **"I'm not good at that." "I'm not ready." "People like me don't**.*"* You're not trapped by reality—you're trapped by repetition.

Picture the room you've built. The walls are tall, but they aren't concrete; they're beliefs you rehearsed until they felt like facts. At first the circle feels kind. It keeps out embarrassment, risk, failure. Then one day you realize it kept out growth, too. Safety and stagnation wear the same mask. Comfort tells you, **"You're fine."** Peace tells you, **"You can rise."** One tucks you in. The other wakes you up.

Most people stay because the familiar hurts less than the unknown. Our brains are wired to protect us from threats—and anything new feels threatening. So we shrink our lives to fit our fear and call it wisdom. We build routines that lower the volume on anxiety, and then wonder why we can't hear our calling. We say we're **"stuck,"** but most of the time we're misaligned: goals that say one thing, habits that do another. You can't claim you want a bigger life while training your nervous system to avoid every stretch.

Here's the flip: the walls were never built to last. They're stories—and stories can be edited. The first crack isn't heroic; it's honest. Stand in the middle of your room and say the thing you've been dodging: I made these walls. I maintained them. And because I built them, I can unbuild them. That sentence is a sledgehammer.

This is where **the Circle of Growth** begins—not with hustle, but with truth. You stop performing and start practicing. You stop asking for permission and start choosing alignment. You run one loop, not your whole life at once: tell the truth about where you are; pick one real priority; make one decision that matches your values; measure one thing that matters; finish one hard thing you said you would. It's not glamorous, but it's freedom in work clothes. Each pass through the loop is another brick loosened, another inch of sky.

Don't confuse ownership with self-blame. Ownership says, **"I built this, so I can rebuild it."** That's power. And don't confuse self-focus with selfishness, either. Choosing growth isn't abandoning people; it's refusing to abandon yourself. The people you're called to lead don't need your comfort—they need your clarity.

If you need a picture, use this: every excuse is mortar; every aligned action is daylight. Comfort will keep offering you silence—no risk, no stretch, no change. Peace will keep offering you a mirror. Look. Are your actions reflecting your purpose or your fear? Are you living, or just maintaining? When the answers sting, you're close. Clarity makes excuses uncomfortable.

You don't escape the comfort zone by leaping over the wall. You walk out through a door you forgot you installed. You try again where you once quit. You speak up where you went quiet. You risk "**looking new**" at something and let the awkwardness do its job: teach you. The circle loosens. Air moves. Possibility shows up like light under a door.

Here's the promise: what waits beyond comfort isn't chaos—it's capacity. Not a life without fear, but a life where fear stops setting your calendar. The Circle of Growth won't beg you to be fearless; it will train you to be faithful: faithful to the truth, to the work, to the next right step. One brick at a time.

You were not built to die safe. You were built to live significant. If you're ready, start here. Stop rehearsing your fears. Start rehearsing your faith. The wall remembers the hands that made it. It'll recognize yours when you take it down.

The Adversity Zone — the second stage of growth, where comfort ends and character starts.

Leaving the comfort zone feels brave for about five minutes. Then you hit the weather. Not a brick wall—paper. Thin, sneaky, everywhere. Every step forward stings like a paper cut: the awkward first rep, the resume you finally send, the rejection that lands ten minutes later, the plan that looked clean in your head and messy in real life. None of it is fatal. All of it is irritating. And that's the trap—because irritation tempts you to run back to "**safe.**" But this isn't death. It's birth. You're not being torn down; you're being formed.

Adversity is a fog, not a map. You can't see far. You can't predict the next slice. You feel it as you move: the ego flare when you look new at something, the quiet shame after a miss, the story in your head that says, "**See? This is why we stay small.**" That story is the real pain. The cut fades. The story lingers—unless you choose a different one. In the Adversity Zone, the choice is simple, not easy: keep walking, or keep circling.

Here's the shift no one advertises: the more you face the cuts, the less they hurt. Not because life gets softer, but because you get stronger. You stop interpreting every "**no**" as a verdict and start treating it like data. You stop bargaining with your old limits and start budgeting for discomfort the way you budget for rent. Rejection becomes a rep. Delay becomes conditioning. Silence becomes focus.

The world didn't lighten up; your nervous system leveled up.

You'll want to retreat. Of course you will. Your brain is wired to avoid uncertainty. But the comfort you miss is the same thing that muted you. Safety and stagnation are twins; they just dress different. If you go back, you trade the sting of progress for the ache of regret. If you stay, you trade the thrill of shortcuts for the confidence of capacity. Pick your pain.

This is also where honesty stops being optional. Adversity exposes your defaults. Visionaries default to ideas and try to outrun hard steps with bigger dreams. Implementers default to steps and try to outrun risk with perfect plans. Neither is wrong, and neither is enough. The fog forces calibration. If you're heavy on vision, you learn cadence—one priority, one experiment, one metric that matters. If you're heavy on implementation, you practice altitude—lifting your head long enough to ensure the ladder is on the right wall. Adversity is not just testing your effort; it's tuning your engine.

And alignment matters here more than ever. When you're moving through paper, the wrong path shreds you faster. Know your lane—Contributor, Independent Creator, Visionary Builder, Strategic Investor—so your grind matches your design. The wrong environment will make ordinary adversity feel catastrophic. The right environment will make the same cuts feel like training. It's not about escaping pain; it's about choosing pain with a payoff.

So how do you actually move? Not with drama— with rhythm. Run the Circle. Tell the truth about where you are. Take one clean step. Measure what actually happened. Adjust without ego. Repeat. You're not trying to crash through the fog; you're learning to navigate in it. One clear promise kept is stronger than ten motivational speeches. One finished rep is louder than twenty intentions. Keep score with actions, not adjectives.

You'll know you're crossing the zone when the same cuts stop hijacking your day. The first rejection used to spiral you for a week; now it costs you an hour. The first awkward attempt used to make you disappear; now you post the second attempt before lunch. That's what resilience looks like in real time—not a cape, just a shorter recovery window. You're building shock absorbers.

Adversity also cleans your circle. People who only loved your comfort won't love your stretch. Let them be uncomfortable somewhere else. You don't need applause to persist. You need alignment to proceed. Protect your headspace like it's oxygen—because in this zone, it is.

Final truth: the paper never stops being paper. It stays thin and annoying. You change. You stop bleeding over small slices. You stop shrinking to avoid them. You stop telling yourself that irritation equals injury. And on a random Tuesday, you realize the thing that used to send you running is now just... Tuesday. That's the crossing.

If you're in it right now—good. That means you left the cage. Keep moving. Cut by cut. Lesson by lesson. Not around it—through it. The Adversity Zone isn't here to end you; it's here to edit you. On the other side is the next version of you—the one with capacity, not just intent; receipts, not just hype.

This is stage two of **the Circle of Growth**. Walk it like you were built for it. Because you are.

The Zone of Growth — where purpose becomes your pattern.

And yeah, it's cyclical. Some weeks feel like a highlight reel. Others feel like you're back in the fog, bumping your shins on the same furniture. But if you're paying attention, your recovery time is shrinking. You bounce faster. You course-correct sooner. You don't spiral for a week over what you can fix in an afternoon. That's capacity—not louder motivation, tighter muscle.

In this zone, comparison is noise. Your path won't look like mine, and it shouldn't. Your success might be leading a team through a tough quarter, finally shipping the thing you've been "**working on,**" or building systems that let you be present for your real life. All valid. Growth is personal, but it isn't private—your consistency feeds your circle. The way you show up gives other people permission to rise.

The Circle of Growth stays the engine. You keep running the loop: tell the truth, set a direction, line up support, simplify the work, choose values over vibes, measure what matters, execute with discipline. Then again. And again. Not because you're broken, but because you're building brick by brick, habit by habit, choice by choice.

Here's the part I want you to tattoo on your mindset: you control exactly two levers—who you are and what you do next. Pull them on purpose. If today feels like adversity, cool—name it and adjust. If today feels like momentum, excellent—protect it and repeat. Either way, you're in motion, and motion—aligned motion—wins.

And yeah, it's cyclical. Some weeks feel like a highlight reel. Others feel like you're back in the fog, bumping your shins on the same furniture. But if you're paying attention, your recovery time is shrinking. You bounce faster. You course-correct sooner. You don't spiral for a week over what you can fix in an afternoon. That's capacity—not louder motivation, tighter muscle.

In this zone, comparison is noise. Your path won't look like mine, and it shouldn't. Your success might be leading a team through a tough quarter, finally shipping the thing you've been "**working on**," or building systems that let you be present for your real life. All valid. Growth is personal, but it isn't private—your consistency feeds your circle. The way you show up gives other people permission to rise.

The Circle of Growth stays the engine. You keep running the loop: tell the truth, set a direction, line up support, simplify the work, choose values over vibes, measure what matters, execute with discipline. Then again. And again. Not because you're broken, but because you're building brick by brick, habit by habit, choice by choice.

Here's the part I want you to tattoo on your mindset: you control exactly two levers—who you are and what you do next. Pull them on purpose. If today feels like adversity, cool—name it and adjust. If today feels like momentum, excellent—protect it and repeat. Either way, you're in motion, and motion—aligned motion—wins.

So welcome to the Zone of Growth. No confetti. No final boss. Just the quiet satisfaction of keeping your promises to yourself, and watching your life get heavier with evidence.

You're not chasing a moment anymore—you're building a legacy in real time.

This is where purpose meets execution. This is where your results stop looking lucky and start looking inevitable. Keep the rhythm. Keep the receipts. You're not done—you're dialed in.

Part IV

Leadership Operating System

Interlude: The Journey IV — Context Over Clout

Monday's market board meets in the back of the firehouse, where the coffee tastes like penance and the chairs never forgive. Attendance is half vendors, half volunteers, and one sheriff who looks allergic to minutes.

"New signage created a bottleneck," says a man in a camo cap, flipping through printed photos as if they're crime evidence. "Folks queued into my stall's airspace."

Nova, composed to the eyelashes, leans forward. "We rotated the arrow. The queue now curves, not collides."

"It *was* worse before," Mrs. Ramirez offers, steady as a metronome. "I sold out early. That never happens this side of Easter."

Priya slides a single paper across the table. One page, three charts, four sentences. "Before → After," she says. "Pauses increased. Questions decreased. Adjacent stall kept flow. We adjusted tape placement at 11:12 a.m. Result: no collisions. We're proposing five more pilot signs, paid by a micro-grant."

The board—wary but curious—reads. The sheriff sips and nods once. "Plain English," he says, which in Briarcliff is a vote.

They approve two hundred dollars and a stern caution about not "Disney-fying" the market. Nova smiles as if awarded a medal for restraint. Yeshua keeps his mouth shut and lets the results do the talking.

Let results speak before you do.

Tuesday is rehearsal day, but not the theater kind. Nova runs a "pre-mortem" in the makerspace, her voice the efficient clip of someone who's broken enough things to respect friction.

"Trial day will go sideways," she says. "We choose *which* sideways."

She deals index cards like a blackjack dealer with an agenda: PRINTER JAM, CLIENT LATE, COLOR-BLIND TESTER FAILS RED/GREEN PALETTE, LAST-MINUTE FIRE EXIT REGULATION. Kyrie adds one: WRONG ARROW DIRECTION. Priya adds: BUDGET CUTS MID-MEETING. Zee adds: MIC HUM, VIDEO FILE CORRUPT.

They run drills. Yeshua labels folders, preps black-white alternates, designs icons that read even if the world were gray. Kyrie forces every arrow to earn its direction with a shout test: "You're ten feet away. Which way do you walk?" If anyone hesitates, the arrow goes to remedial.

By afternoon, Yeshua can feel the outline of the studio he hasn't seen. He can also feel the fatigue of preparation done right. He packs his bag like a pilot: tools, backups, a spare shirt, and a small index card on top that reads: **Loop, not legend.**

Rehearse breaking points, not just best case.

Wednesday's trial day at Foundry East unfolds with a professional kind of chaos—polite, caffeinated, non-apologetic. The studio lives in an old printing warehouse—high windows, concrete floors that remember winters, walls punctured with cork boards dense as forests.

A woman with a streak of silver in her hair and a walk that means business introduces herself. "Mara Quinn. Principal. Welcome. Your brief is not hypothetical." She gestures to a floor plan. "Pop-up health clinic. Three hours. Wayfinding must work for seniors, parents juggling toddlers, and volunteers who don't read maps. The fire marshal will check exits. If your arrows lie, he'll find them."

She pairs Yeshua with two other trialists: Luca—sharp jawline, sharper skepticism—and Gia—quiet, eyes like a good camera.

They split zones, assign responsibilities, and set a fifteen-minute standup rhythm. It's a dance. It's also a gauntlet.

First pass is too pretty. The clinic coordinator—a woman in scrubs and relentless kindness—stops at a sign and squints. "Where's 'Check-In'?"

"Right there," Luca says, proud.

She smiles. "You hid it."

They strip the flourish. Second pass gets the labels right but misreads the room—two parents with strollers face an impossible left turn. Gia finds them before frustration can grow a voice, pivots the sign, and changes the flow like water finding a slope.

Third pass nearly works until an older man with a slow gait points his cane at a green arrow and says, "Can't see it." Yeshua breathes once, drops to black-white and icon-first, and retests. The man nods. "Better," he says. "My eyes are honest about being tired."

By noon, the system stands: high-contrast labels, pictograms that carry their own weight, arrows that anticipate clogs. The fire marshal looks disappointed that nothing is obviously wrong, then finds a too-low sign and frowns in relief. "Raise it six inches," he says. They do.

Mara walks the hallway slow, like a detective who lets the room confess. "You," she says to Yeshua, "expose your thinking fast and cheap. Keep that. You recover in public without drama. Keep that more."

He nods, adrenaline finally leaning toward fatigue.

"We take two trialists for a sixty-day placement," Mara continues. "We'll call tonight."

Luca's jaw unknots a fraction. Gia meets Yeshua's eyes and gives the smallest of nods—solidarity without speech.

As the room decompresses, Yeshua notices a silver cufflink on the floor, out of place among tape scraps and old staples. He pockets it absentmindedly, intending to hand it to the front desk. He will forget to until later, which is the sort of detail that means nothing—until it doesn't.

Fall in small, recover in public.

On the bus back, his phone vibrates with a message from an unfamiliar number.

YD—Assistant to Malik. We're cutting clips from Spotlight Hour. Malik wants to include your "Two Case Studies" in a sizzle. Clean credit. Zero fee. Big reach. Cool?

A second text arrives before he formulates the second half of a thought.

Also: scholarship applications open. Malik asked me to flag you for an interview slot. No pressure, just doors.

He rewrites his rule on the inside of his head: **Proof—then spotlight. Spiral up, not out.** Then he types:

Use the clip if it links to the full case study post with numbers. No adjectives, no claims I didn't make. I'm not applying yet. Building muscle.

The typing dots appear, disappear, return like someone rehearsing a tone. Finally: *Respect. Sending to the edit team. Door stays open.*

He pockets the phone and watches Briarcliff roll by—lawns, porches, the faded billboard near the highway that still advertises a Fourth of July two years gone. Everyone here lives with a version of the past. He intends to live with a version of the future.

Thursday at the makerspace, they do what most crews forget after a "big day": they write the play so someone else can run it.

Nova draws a clean, brutal checklist on the whiteboard:

1. Walk the space.
2. Mark friction (people, not theory).
3. Draft ugly.
4. Test on feet older than yours.
5. Strip the pretty, keep the clear.
6. Retest under constraint (time, weather, noise).
7. Document like a bored accountant.
8. Post the proof.
9. Archive the lesson.
10. Pay people on time.

Priya turns it into a one-pager that looks like it would survive court. Kyrie hangs a laminated copy near the exit with a label maker's gravitas. Zee films a two-minute "how we" with voiceover that sounds like a gentle recipe.

"Tiny franchise," Nova says, satisfied. "If we go on vacation or break an ankle, this still runs."

Write the play so others can run it.

Hale stops by with coffee and a look that—on him—counts as effusive. "My chairs breed at night now," he says. "I put down a deposit on another load of white oak, against the advice of my inner accountant."

"Buy oak like you mean it," Priya tells him, then adds, "but let me look at your cashflow."

He writes his email on a folded receipt and slides it across like contraband.

Friday takes its weather personally. Power flickers by 10:00 a.m. By 10:30, the market half-opens, half-refuses. Battery lights bloom like stubborn stars under tents. The PA system coughs and quits.

At 11:05, a small voice becomes a big problem. "Owen?" a woman calls, calm on a hair trigger. "Owen!"

The market tightens—eyes up, conversations paused, the hum of a community bracing. Kyrie is moving before anyone assigns him a job, scanning paths and crouching to kids' eye level. Nova prints **HELP DESK →** in block letters on the back of a failed poster and tapes it to the information table. Priya starts a log: time last seen, shirt color, shoes, comfort item (stuffed llama), mother's number.

Zee rolls quietly, camera down at hip level to avoid turning panic into content. "No faces," they murmur, as if promising the room it won't be exploited.

Yeshua climbs onto a stable chair (tested) and lets his voice find the right distance. "We're looking for Owen," he says into the dead PA's ancient fallback: air. "Red shirt, blue shoes, stuffed llama. We're setting a **Help Desk** at info. If you see him, bring him there. If you're with children, stay where you are so they don't chase you in circles."

The market obeys—not because he commands but because the plan is obvious. A volunteer jogs the perimeter with a walkie that currently has the confidence of a paperweight. Kyrie stations himself at the restroom bottleneck. Nova marks an X on the ground near info where any sighting report goes first.

Six minutes later—six eternal minutes—Tino (oil-change apprentice turned crowd-scanner) appears with a small boy holding a very damp llama. Owen looks unimpressed by crisis, as children often do when the world forgets they have internal maps.

The mother sobs once, then laughs. The room exhales in one of those communal breaths that makes towns worth the compromise.

They don't make a speech. They write it down: **In chaos, downgrade ambition, upgrade coordination.** Priya adds a "Lost Child Protocol" to the market binder. Nova adds a line to the sign kit: HELPDESK arrows pre-printed. Kyrie tests the tape in rain and writes the brand on the box.

When the power returns in a stuttering apology, an older woman from the historical society pats Yeshua's forearm with a hand that has seen wars and weddings. "You made it simple," she says. "Simple saves."

In chaos, downgrade ambition, upgrade coordination.

Saturday morning brings two things: a front-page mention above the fold—*"Quick Action, Clear Signs Help Reunite Child at Market"*—and a DM from Malik, remarkably human without the sheen.

Saw the clip in the paper. Good leadership. No glitz. Proud of the town. And of you for not turning it into a selfie.

He doesn't reply. There's nothing to say that wouldn't tilt the balance.

At noon, Foundry East calls. Mara's voice is matter-of-fact with a thread of pleased surprise woven through.

"Yeshua," she says. "You recover well. You notice boring things, which is where systems hide. Sixty-day placement. Starts Monday. Stipend is... not terrible. We'll teach you to ask better questions. We'll also ask you to fail faster than your comfort."

He says yes before she finishes the last sentence.

"Bring your loop," she says, and hangs up like a person who has somewhere to be.

He stands in the small kitchen, the linoleum honestly cracked, the sink clean from habit. He allows a laugh—the unguarded kind that makes rooms feel bigger from the inside.

Lucía appears, reading his face like a monitor. "Well?"

"They're taking me," he says.

She wraps him in a hug that forgives three years of stagnation with one squeeze. "Good," she says into his shoulder. "My boy is building something that will not fall when the weather changes."

He breathes out a promise into the fabric of her scrubs: **If it doesn't stand in the rain, it doesn't belong in your plan.**

They meet that evening at Rosie's—the booth claiming them like a ritual. Kyrie slides a small box across the table. Inside: a label maker and three rolls of tape, industrial grade.

"Promotion package," he says. "For your feelings."

Nova produces a notebook with "PLAYS" embossed on the cover in foil that looks more expensive than it was. "Write down your favorite failures," she says. "They'll be shy later."

Priya passes a manila folder—"Payroll, taxes, and things the government expects even from geniuses." It's color-coded only enough to keep a person honest.

Zee hands him a flash drive in a tiny case. On the label: **Mateo—Evidence Reel**. "One minute," they say. "Cut like a police report. If anyone asks what you do, *show* that."

He looks at this improbable little crew and realizes he has built an operating system out of people—each one a subroutine that makes him better, faster, more honest. In a kinder book, that would be the end of the chapter.

This isn't that book.

Because when they step into the evening—air washed clean by recent rain, neon buzzing its small song—Yeshua notices a new poster on the community board beside the door. The silver ink catches what's left of daylight, which is exactly its point.

DRAVEN x BRIARCLIFF—COMMUNITY PARTNERSHIP NIGHT: "TURN YOUR TOWN INTO A BRAND."

Below it, in smaller letters you only catch if you lean: *Featuring local builders.* A list follows. His name is not on it. Hale's is. So is Mrs. Ramirez's. So is Alvarez Auto.

A detail: the font weight on "Community Partnership" is heavier than "Night." Another: the sponsor line at the bottom is the same as the cufflink pattern he pocketed at Foundry East.

He touches his pocket and feels the small metal oval he forgot to return. A coincidence is a staircase that may or may not lead somewhere. Agatha would smile here and not warn anyone.

"Are we featured?" Nova asks, reading fast.

"Not by name," Priya says, nose wrinkling.

Kyrie taps the list with a finger as calm as a gavel. "He can invite whoever he wants," he says. "We can attend—or not. But these are our people."

Yeshua looks at the names: the very folks they've been helping, pulled toward a stage that may pay in applause and invoices neither of them wrote. He hears Malik's not-wrong counsel in one ear and their unglamorous loop in the other. Then he hears his mother's sentence—*Name the risk, honor it, then act anyway*—and it lines up the room.

"Let's go," he says. "Not to perform. To protect. To make sure the mirror doesn't become a mask."

Nova grins, wolfish. "I do love a field trip."

Priya tucks the poster's details into her calendar like a blade. Kyrie sets a reminder to bring the wrench that solves more than cars. Zee checks their battery and says nothing, which is the loudest thing they do.

They walk into a night that is not dramatic, exactly—but full of the small suspense that precedes honest work. Somewhere, a silver cufflink waits to be claimed. Somewhere else, a room is being measured for mirrors.

Introduction to Growth

Leading is hard because too many leaders stop at slogans.

Values get posted; they don't get practiced. **The Circle of Growth** fixes that. It's a straight-up operating system for leadership that links who you are to what you do—so your character shows up in your calendar, your meetings, and your results. You run it as a simple loop: get clear, act, learn, adjust, repeat. Each pass turns clarity into action, action into outcomes, and outcomes into improvement. No fluff. No "**poster values**." Just patterns that work.

Beneath the hood are **seven core traits** paired with **seven matching actions**—your inner game wired to your outer habits. That pairing becomes a **workflow (the 7Ps)** you can drop into any *team* or *organization*. It gives you crisp priorities, owners, checklists, and a handful of hard metrics—so people move faster, friction drops and wins compound.

This isn't theory. It's how new managers find their footing, how nonprofit founders scale impact, how executives align cross-functional chaos, and how veterans turn discipline into momentum in civilian life. If you can run a loop, you can lead with intention—and prove it.

Where character becomes execution.

What this is (and why it matters)

Most strategies don't fail because leaders are lazy—they fail because "**who you are**" never gets translated into "**what you do.**" Studies routinely show a painful gap between plans and shipped results. **The Circle of Growth** closes that gap by linking inner character to outer execution in a simple, repeatable loop.

The core idea

The Circle of Growth pairs seven Traits (**who we are**) with seven Actions (**what we do**), organized across seven business workflow (**the 7 Ps**). You run the loop in short cycles—weeks and quarters—so clarity becomes action, action becomes results, and results start compounding.

- Tight mapping: **Trait → Action → Workflow**
- **Short cycles**: weekly focus + quarterly review
- **Evidence of progress:** a small scorecard you actually use
- **Tool-agnostic:** layers over *OKRs, Agile, SOPs, CRM*—no rip-and-replace

The canonical mapping

- *Purpose*: **Self-Awareness → Assess** → establish the why/where before spending
- *People*: **Courage → Clarify** → make direction, priorities, and roles undeniable
- *Product:* **Humility → Harness** → align strengths, tools, timing; remove friction
- *Process*: **Integrity → Innovate** → improve how value is created (bold, values-aligned)

- ***Principles***: **Empathy** → **Empower** → operationalize values; grow others with trust
- ***Performance***: **Learning** → **Validate** → instrument outcomes; adjust based on evidence
- ***Profit***: **Execution** → **Execute** → deliver reliably; protect margins; reinvest well

The operating behaviors (Traits & Actions) and the 7 Ps

The 7 Traits (who you are)

- ***Self-Awareness*** — You see your drivers and impact; course-correct early.
- ***Courage*** — You make truth safe; small problems surface while they're still small.
- ***Humility*** — You keep the system smarter than any one person; ideas flow.
- ***Integrity*** — You do what's right without an audience; trust becomes the default.
- ***Empathy*** — You lead humans, not headcount; safety and ownership grow.
- ***Learning*** — You unlearn fast and adjust; reality has a seat at the table.
- ***Execution*** — You finish; strategy turns into shipments, not slideware.

The 7 Actions (what you do)

- ***Assess*** — Start with truth. Baseline, risks, assumptions, owners.

- ***Clarify*** — Name outcomes, priorities, and roles in plain language.
- ***Harness*** — Focus people/time/tools; limit WIP; kill context-switching.
- ***Innovate*** — Upgrade the way you create value; small bets, fast learning.
- ***Empower*** — Delegate with guardrails; recognize wins; widen access.
- ***Validate*** — Measure few real outcomes; review on cadence; adapt.
- ***Execute*** — Ship to definition-of-done; protect quality and margins.

Workflow

The 7 Ps (where it applies)

- ***Purpose*** — Direction and success criteria
- ***People*** — Talent, trust, and collaboration
- ***Product*** — Value that actually solves a problem
- ***Process*** — Reliable flow that beats heroics
- ***Principles*** — Ethics, standards, and governance
- ***Performance*** — Goals, metrics, and reviews
- ***Profit*** — Resilient economics that fund the next loop

Core artifacts (by Action)

- ***Assess:*** one-page baseline, risks & responsibilities, owner map
- ***Clarify:*** outcome statement, priority list, decision log, role grid

- ***Harness***: strengths/role matrix, resource plan, blocker board
- ***Innovate:*** hypothesis card, tiny prototype, change log/SOP update
- ***Empower***: recognition log, delegation thresholds, reinvestment plan
- ***Validate:*** scorecard (few metrics), review notes, next-step commitments
- ***Execute:*** cadence calendar, WIP limits, definition-of-done checklist

Cadence (keep it light and real)

- **Weekly (30–45 min):**
1. What mattered?
2. What shipped?
3. What's blocked?
4. What's next?
- **Monthly (60–90 min):**
- **Quarterly (2–3 hrs):**

Re-Assess purpose & context; re-Clarify 3–5 outcomes; re-Harness resources.

Review scorecard; retire a failing bet; double-down on one winner.

Measurement (few signals, not a dashboard zoo)

- ***Leading indicators***: clarity of priorities, cycle time, blocker age, adoption/usage

- **Lagging indicators**: quality/defects, goal attainment, retention, margin/reserves
- **Visibility**: one shared scorecard, one owner per metric, one review rhythm

Applications

Weeks 1–2 — Stand-up
90-day quick start

- **Individuals**: self-management, habit systems, career momentum
- **Teams**: alignment, cleaner handoffs, predictable delivery, continuous improvement
- **Organizations**: strategy execution, culture reinforcement, portfolio focus
- Run *Assess*: one-page baseline + risks; name owners.
- Run *Clarify*: choose 3 outcomes; define done; publish roles.
- Set weekly/quarterly rhythms on the calendar.
- Run *Harness*: focus work; limit WIP; public blocker board.
- Run *Innovate*: 1–2 tiny bets to improve how value is created.
- Start *Validate*: ship small changes; measure, learn, adjust.
- Run *Empower*: delegate with guardrails; recognize wins; share access.
- Run *Execute*: protect quality margins; close the loop on definition-of-done.

- Quarterly review: retire what failed; fund what performed.

Relation to other methods (plug-and-play)

Circle of Growth complements *OKRs, Agile, Lean, and balanced* scorecards. It supplies the **identity-to-behavior** link and the **loop** that keeps those systems honest and effective.

Guardrails (what this isn't)

This framework does not replace *industry regulations, safety standards, or specialized compliance*. Results depend on leadership commitment, psychological safety, and the discipline to review and adjust on cadence.

Part V

Scaling Growth

Interlude: The Journey V — How the Leader Operating System works

They don't go to "Community Partnership Night" dressed for war. They go dressed for work. Nova in black jeans and a jacket with too many pockets. Priya with a clipboard the color of good decisions. Kyrie in a clean Alvarez Auto polo because he still has a shift later. Zee wearing a camera as if it's a passport, not a weapon. Yeshua with a flat pack of letter-size papers in his bag titled, without drama: **Context Agreements**.

Rosie's neon hums at their backs as they cross Main. The auditorium's glass doors reflect Briarcliff the way a mirror reflects intention—accurately, if you stand still long enough. Inside, volunteers hand out programs with a silver logo that matches the tiny pattern on the cufflink in Yeshua's pocket. A detail. A thread.

Hale stands near the stage, jacket too formal for a man who prefers sawdust, looking like a tree introduced at a cocktail party. Mrs. Ramirez wears her market apron on purpose. Alvarez's foreman, Marta, leans against a column as if columns were invented for leaning.

"Evening," Hale says, relief palpable when he spots them—like a man who sees his level bubble centered. "They want me to 'share my brand narrative.' I told them I sell chairs."

"Say that," Nova advises. "Then sit in one."

Yeshua draws Hale aside, offers a single sheet. "If anyone shows numbers, ask them to read this line aloud," he says, tapping the clause on the **Context Agreement**. *Any use of results must include the time window, the intervention, and the baseline.* "It keeps the mirror from lying."

Hale scans, nods, folds the paper with the care he gives to dovetails. Mrs. Ramirez tucks hers into her apron like a prayer card. Marta reads and smirks. "Bless you," she says. "People love to quote us without paying us."

On stage, a tasteful projection: **DRAVEN x BRIARCLIFF—TURN YOUR TOWN INTO A BRAND**. The word *brand* is heavy; the rest of the sentence bows under it.

The assistant—YD on texts, "Yvette Devon" on the name badge—glides over. "Lovely to have local builders," she says in a voice that files the edges off words.

"Lovely to define terms," Priya replies, smiling. "We're sharing proof, not myth."

Yvette's eyes flick, clocking the hazard. "Right. Of course. We're aligned on authenticity." The last word lands like a marble on linoleum.

They take seats halfway back, not hiding, not begging for spotlight. Malik enters without the earlier theater—no fog, no swell—just crisp timing and a white shirt that photographs well. The room quiets. He doesn't wave it quiet; it gives him the hush like a gift he has earned or stolen. He opens with town history, not himself. Smart. Disarming.

He speaks clean. He says, "A brand is just behavior other people recognize," and Priya underlines that line in her program twice. He says, "You cannot post your way around a bad process," and Nova gives him one grudging eyebrow of respect. He says, "Our job here is to make the right thing the easy thing," and Kyrie's mouth tics at the corner.

Then the panel begins.

Hale is first, flanked by a slide that shows his window—today's third iteration, the sentence short and muscular. The lower-third graphic reads: *HALE THOMAS — WHITE OAK CHAIRMAKER*. Hale clears his throat, finds his own cadence.

"I made lovely things and hid them," he says. "We put the price where eyes could see it. Sales followed. I believe this is called math." Laughter lands, honest.

The next slide appears—before/after bars. Yeshua's stomach tightens at once. The numbers are right. The caption isn't. It says: *"Brand Lab intervention increases sales."*

He stands without standing, voice halfway to the aisle. "Context," he says—soft, but it travels. "Please add 'window sign and price visibility implemented by shop owner with local crew.'" He isn't performing; he is adjusting a crooked frame.

Hale turns to the screen. "Aye," he says simply. "Add that. We did that together."

Silence thinks. Then Malik says, into his mic, "Note it." The A/V tech types. The caption changes, pennies of truth dropping into a jar. **Always fix the label before you fix the lighting.**

Mrs. Ramirez speaks next. She wants no slide, only the board itself, which someone has lugged in at her request. She taps it. "This told the truth faster than my mouth," she says. "People bought jam because I let them read."

Marta follows with a story about directing intake flow during a storm—three arrows, two volunteers, one stubborn door. She says the word *voltage* when she means momentum and nobody corrects her because it feels right.

Then, between panels, the sizzle reel rolls. Zee tenses. The first seconds are clean—jars, feet, arrows. Then: a montage that tips toward fable. Yeshua's voice, clipped from the Spotlight Hour, patched under footage he doesn't recognize. The lower-third flashes a hashtag. A thin layer of sugar forms.

Zee leans to Yeshua. "Want me to cut their feed?" It's a joke, mostly.

He stands at the mic placed in the aisle for "audience engagement." He waits for a breath that isn't borrowed. "Can we add links to the full posts with numbers?" he asks. "The story is the steps. The steps live where we wrote them down."

Malik looks at the A/V table; the tech—bless all underpaid techs—even shrugs like a man ready to copy-paste truth. "Do it," Malik says.

Yvette's smile does not slip; it freezes. "We'll update in post," she calls as if the room is a camera that will take directions.

"Now," Malik says, not unkind. "Context loses power when it ships late." He turns to the room. "This is the only fight that's worth anything: proof versus polish. We will choose proof."

No one claps. That's good. They're listening.

When the room wants a story, give it a system.

During the break, a man with a banker's tie and the sponsor's logo on his lapel approaches. The cufflink in Yeshua's pocket hums with coincidence.

"Trent Vale," the man says, extending a hand. "Vale & Rist Marketing. We underwrite the Brand Lab. We loved your segment last week. Very… grounded."

"Your cufflinks are handsome," Yeshua says lightly. "One of them is visiting with me." He pulls the small silver oval from his pocket. Trent blinks once too slow.

"Foundry East," Yeshua adds, returning the cufflink. "On the floor after a trial day. Either you attended or your friend did."

Trent recovers. "We collaborate widely," he says. "Small world."

"Small towns," Nova corrects, and offers her card with *PLAYS* stamped on it like a verdict. "We'll license our checklists if you fund micro-grants with strings attached to data, not to clout."

Trent chuckles. He is the sort who speaks chuckle. "Ambitious."

"Specific," Priya says, already sliding the one-pager across. *Clarity Commons Micro-Grant Pilot.* Bullet points like rail ties: $5,000 split five ways; pay vendors; post proof; open template; no exclusivity; one monthly clinic for Foundry East or equivalent to train locals. Yeshua watches the man's eyes track cost before benefit. He does the same math with different weights.

Trent pockets the paper as if it were a receipt. "We'll review."

"Review fast," Kyrie says, gentle but firm. "Momentum's clock runs on batteries, not calendars."

Negotiate terms when the room still remembers why it gathered.

The second half of the night shifts from show to ask. A young volunteer from the food pantry describes how "Turn your town into a brand" sounds like "Turn the people into a product" if you don't add guardrails. Zee records from the hip, framing hands and paper, not faces.

Finally, Malik returns to the center. "We'll end with this," he says. "A pledge."

The screen lights up: *The Context Pledge*. A short set of sentences. Proof before spotlight. Baseline and window on every slide. No exclusivity on community data. Pay the people whose stories you use.

It's not performative; it's procedural. He raises a hand. "If you build here, I invite you to sign it."

Hale signs, pen heavy. Mrs. Ramirez signs like a woman who has signed deeds and school slips and a letter once to a son overseas. Marta signs with a mechanic's pressure. Nova signs, precise. Priya signs next to a note: *Metrics matter*. Kyrie writes his name with a speed that matches his gait. Zee draws a tiny camera icon under their initials.

Yeshua waits. He considers the room, the mirror, the mask, the man in the white shirt who both threatens and protects. He signs. Then he adds five words at the bottom, small and stubborn:

Run the loop—then run it again.

Malik reads it, then looks up—an expression that says both *I see you* and *I am not finished testing you.* He nods once.

Choose the pledge that limits your future celebrity and expands your future capacity.

After the crowd thins, Malik steps down from the stage and stands where conversations pool. He addresses Yeshua the way he addressed him after the Spotlight—plain.

"You fought the sizzle," he says. "Good."

"You fixed the caption," Yeshua counters. "Also good."

They study each other a fraction of a second too long. "You're building a commons," Malik says. "You'll need enemies to keep it honest—and friends to keep it safe. Don't mix the two."

Yeshua considers a question he's been carrying like a coin. "Why didn't you put my name on the poster?"

Malik's mouth quirks. "I wanted to know if you'd come anyway."

"And if I hadn't?"

"Then I would've known which kind of builder you were."

"Which kind is that?"

"The kind who only shows up when his name is printed."

Yeshua hums, conceding the test and disliking it all at once. "Don't run this experiment often," he says. "It breaks trust."

"Duly noted," Malik says. "Some failures don't improve with repetition."

They shake hands like men who do not plan to become each other but plan to take each other seriously.

Outside, the air holds the kind of cool that helps thoughts set. They walk past the poster, now annotated with a pen—someone has added *PROOF INSIDE* under the QR code. Nova grins. "Street designer at work," she says.

"Tomorrow," Priya says, "we turn this pledge into a page and that page into a practice."

"And that practice into a kit," Kyrie adds. "And that kit into stock."

Zee lifts the lens one last time, catching them not as heroes but as silhouettes in a town that now knows a rule it can keep.

Systems win because they don't require your mood.

Sunday evening, Trent emails first. Short, efficient: *Vale & Rist will fund your pilot if Foundry East co-signs. No exclusivity. Reports monthly. Good faith on both sides.*

Mara follows less than an hour later: *Consider it co-signed. Your loop meets our threshold. Don't let the money boss you around. Start Monday.*

They answer as a crew: one sentence each, stitched.

Priya: *Budget posted; transparency link attached.*
Nova: *Kit v1.0 printing on Monday; testing Tuesday.*
Kyrie: *Flow audit schedule set; sign-in sheet ready.*
Zee: *Evidence standard: 60 seconds; date; place; numeric claim; no soundtrack.*
Yeshua: *We will run the loop.*

Then he adds the second sentence that makes systems live: *We will teach the loop.*

Teach before you are asked.

Personal Growth

Leadership isn't a title; it's a thermostat. You set the temperature in every room you walk into—by who you are long before what you say. That's why personal growth isn't optional. It's the foundation. If you can't lead yourself on a random Tuesday—when you're tired, busy, and nobody's clapping—why should anyone trust you with their time, budget, or future?

The SCHIELE Method is the inner operating system. ***Seven traits***. Not vibes—behaviors. Live these daily and you don't just improve performance; you change culture. People move different around a leader who's aligned.

Self-Awareness is ground zero. It's knowing your patterns, your tells, your impact. When the team's off, you check the map and the driver. You ask, "How did I land on them?" Then you adjust—tone, timing, expectations. Clear mirrors make cleaner moves.

Courage is motion through discomfort. Not loud, not reckless—honest. You tell the truth sooner, make the call faster, and take the heat when it's yours. Safety isn't the absence of risk; it's the presence of trust. Courage creates that space so people can bring the real problems to the table before they become real fires.

Humility keeps the signal-to-noise ratio low. You're curious, correctable, and generous with credit. No ego tolls at your door. Information flows. The system gets smarter than any one person—especially you.

Integrity is your non-negotiable. You don't bend the rules when it's convenient, and you don't move goalposts when deadlines blink. People can set their watch by your word. That reliability lowers friction and raises speed, because nobody's burning cycles hedging against you.

Empathy is operational. You see people as people, not headcount. You read context, remove blockers, and coach what's actually in front of you. Folks go further for leaders who see them clearly—and stay longer, too.

Learning keeps you adaptable. You turn feedback into fuel, run small experiments, and unlearn fast when reality changes the script. Stagnation is a choice. So is iteration.

Execution is the receipt. Ideas become deliverables. "**Done**" means done—clear scope, owner, and definition of done you can audit. You finish the work, full stop. That's how trust compounds and strategy turns into results.

Why these seven? Because together they close the loop from *character* → *climate* → *outcomes*. Self-awareness sharpens decisions. Courage makes truth tellable. Humility keeps ideas flowing. Integrity stabilizes the field. Empathy powers commitment. Learning accelerates adjustment. Execution makes it real. Miss one, and the rest leak.

Here's the play: weave the seven into your week until they're muscle memory. Check your mirror before you check your metrics. Say the hard thing kindly and quickly. Ask more questions than you answer. Keep your word when it's inconvenient. Lead the human, not just the role. Run one experiment before you rewrite the plan. Ship the thing you promised—on time.

That's ***the SCHIELE Method***. Not philosophy—operations of self. And inside **the Circle of Growth**, these traits don't sit on a poster; they power the rhythm. Who you are becomes what gets done. Consistently. Audibly. Predictably. That's leadership people can feel—and follow.

Professional Development

Professional development isn't extra credit—it's how you get dangerous in the best way. It sharpens how you think, decide, and deliver so your leadership stops being a mood and starts being a machine. **ACHIEVE** is that machine: seven repeatable moves you can run on any project, with any team, in any season—so progress stops being accidental and starts being measurable.

You begin with **Assess**: tell the truth before you tell the plan. Where are we really? What's working, what's wobbling, what's missing? No spin, no slogans—just a clean baseline you can build from. You can't fix what you won't face, and you can't fund what you can't define.

Then **Clarify**: name the target so feet can move. Translate ambition into outcomes, owners, and timing. Direction beats intensity every time. When everyone knows "**what good looks like**," meetings get shorter and momentum stops leaking.

Next is **Harness**: align people, resources, and time to pull as one. You cut the cute work, limit WIP, and point your best energy at the few bets that matter now. This is leadership as force multiplier—less juggling, more finishing, faster cycles.

Now **Innovate**: upgrade the system, not just the output. You run small bets, learn on purpose, and keep values as the guardrails. Bold is only beautiful when it's honest. No theater—just better ways of working that raise the ceiling without breaking the floor.

Then **Empower**: share the stage, grow the choir. You set the "**what**," give room on the "**how**," and make truth tellable. People do their smartest work where it's safe to try, safe to speak, and safe to learn. Authority hoarded is capacity wasted.

After that, **Validate**: trust data over drama. Instrument the work, run the test, keep the wins, cut the misses. Feedback isn't a verdict; it's a velocity boost. Evidence ends the opinion Olympics and puts fuel in the right engines.

Finally, **Execute**: ship. Not vibes, receipts. Clear scope, clear owner, clear "**done**"—and you hit it. Consistency is the ultimate power move because nothing compounds until it's delivered.

String these together and you get a rhythm: *Assess → Clarify → Harness → Innovate → Empower → Validate → Execute*—then loop. The loop is the point. Every pass tightens your aim, speeds your delivery, and deepens trust. Miss one step and the system leaks: skip Assess and you bankroll blind spots; skip Clarify and teams scatter; skip Harness and cycle times swell; skip Innovate and you calcify; skip Empower and candor dries up; skip Validate and you fly by vibes; skip Execute and—well—nothing counts.

So run the play like a pro: start with truth, point the effort, align the muscle, improve the machine, unlock the humans, prove the progress, and finish the work. Do it again next week. That's how strategy stops performing on slides and starts performing in real life. That's how careers grow, teams win, and legacies get built—on purpose.

Weeks 3–6 — Flow & learning

Weeks 7–12 — Scale what work

Workflow

Success isn't magic—it's focus. When you run your work through the **Seven P's,** you stop guessing and start compounding. This is the smallest, tightest set that keeps you grounded, moving, and making real impact.

Purpose.

Start with your why. Aim beats effort. When your goal actually matters to you, it becomes a compass—steady when life gets noisy. Check your week against your why: if the calendar doesn't match the mission, the calendar changes. "**When the why is strong, the how steadies.**" Excellence starts here.

People.

No one wins solo. Choose rooms that raise your ceiling and friends who check your blind spots. Build trust, say the quiet parts out loud, and listen like outcomes depend on it—because they do. The right people multiply your speed and clean up your thinking.

Product.

Make something useful before you make it pretty. Whether it's a service, a program, or your personal craft, quality is your credibility. Ask for feedback early, ship small upgrades often, and keep solving the real problem. When the value's real, word travels.

Process.

How you work determines how far you go. Document the best-known way, simplify the steps, and make progress repeatable. Fewer priorities, clearer handoffs, shorter loops. It's not glamorous—just effective. Systems beat sprints—consistency compounds.

Principles.

Values are your guardrails when the road gets slick. Lead with honesty, empathy, and fairness—especially when it costs you convenience. Decisions get faster and cleaner when you already know what you won't trade.

Performance.

Progress over perfection—every day. Pick a few metrics that matter, review them on a rhythm, and adjust without drama. Let data end debates and turn lessons into your next move. When you measure what matters, momentum shows up.

Profit.

Fuel the mission so the mission can last. Profit is results you can reinvest—money, impact, trust, capacity. Deliver outcomes, protect margins, and put wins back into purpose. Sustainability isn't a vibe; it's stewardship.

Run the loop in order: ***Purpose → People → Product → Process → Principles → Performance → Profit.*** Aim the effort, mobilize the humans, deliver real value, make it flow, keep it trusted, learn on cadence, and fund the next pass.

Do that, and you won't just succeed—you'll build something that lasts.

Scaling Growth Through S.U.M. — *The Visionary Builder*

You've done the inner work. You've aligned who you are with what you do. Now comes the real flex: building a culture that runs without you standing over it. That's the leap from leader to Visionary Builder—from "**I do it**" to "**we do it, reliably**." This is where **the Circle of Growth** extends into **S.U.M.**—*System, Unity, Mastery*—three cultural anchors that turn your personal rhythm into an organizational one. Think of them as stages 8, 9, and 10: the part of the loop that scales.

System — change the rewards, change the behavior.

Most leaders preach collaboration and then quietly reward lone-wolf heroics. Mixed signals = mixed results. System is where you rewire incentives so teamwork isn't a *TED Talk*—it's how you get promoted. Tie recognition and bonuses to shared outcomes. Make cross-functional projects the path to visibility. Design workflows that literally require partnership to finish the job. When the system pays for collaboration, collaboration becomes the standard. Say it with me: you don't just change people—you change what the system rewards.

Unity — build an organizational rhythm that keeps everyone in tune.

Great teams still lose if they play different songs. Unity is deliberate cadence: recurring moments where the whole organism sees itself and moves as one. Hold honest town halls where leaders share wins, misses, and lessons without spin. Run cross-team forums where product, ops, sales, and finance expose dependencies and ask for help. Create shared experiences—service days, internal workshops, lightweight offsites—that remind people, "we're one crew." Alignment isn't a memo; it's a rhythm. Unity makes interdependence visible so silos have nowhere to hide.

Mastery — spread knowledge until it becomes infrastructure.

Hoarded expertise is a ticking time bomb. Mastery means learning compounds because it's shared, not owned. Stand up job shadowing and rotations. Cross-train on critical skills so there's no single point of failure.

Make "**teach what you know**" part of performance—lunch-and-learns, peer workshops, quick playbooks in plain language. Reward people not just for what they ship, but for how many others they level up. That's how you turn talent into bench strength and bench strength into resilience.

Put together, **S.U.M.** turns leadership from personality to operating system. System aligns the incentives. Unity aligns the motion. Mastery aligns the knowledge. Once those three click, your culture starts doing the heavy lifting. Collaboration isn't a campaign—it's how work flows. Transparency isn't a virtue signal—it's the house style. Learning isn't an event—it's the water supply.

Here's how it plays out on the ground. You set a goal that matters (**Purpose**), line up the right people (**People**), deliver something useful (**Product**), make the workflow (**Process**), hold the line on values (**Principles**), learn on cadence (**Performance**), and fund the next pass (**Profit**). Now, **S.U.M.** locks it in at scale:

- *System* converts your talk into teeth. Team-based goals in reviews, cross-functional KPIs on dashboards, rewards that celebrate shared wins—suddenly the fastest path to advancement is helping others succeed.
- *Unity* keeps the signal clean. Leaders model vulnerability, departments share constraints in real time, and the company learns as one organism instead of a pile of departments.
- *Mastery* future-proofs the results. When people rotate, nothing breaks; when someone leaves, the knowledge stays; when the market shifts, your learning muscle is already warm.

None of this is extra credit. It's the difference between short-term momentum and durable lift. Without System, your best intentions drown in misaligned incentives. Without Unity, teams drift and duplicate work. Without Mastery, growth stalls at the speed of your busiest expert.

And yes, this is still **the Circle of Growth**—just zoomed out. The inner traits *(self-awareness, courage, humility, integrity, empathy, learning, execution)* become cultural when **S.U.M.** is in place.

Courage shows up as psychological safety in your town halls. Humility appears as cross-team interest in how others win. Integrity becomes auditable decisions and fair standards. Learning becomes normal, not novel. Execution becomes predictable because the system supports it, not because a hero dragged it across the line.

If you want a quick gut-check, use these prompts:

- *System*: "**Would a rational employee help another team right now and expect it to help their career?**" If the answer is no, fix the incentives.
- *Unity*: "**Where do we regularly see the whole picture together?**" If the only answer is Slack chaos and quarterly all-hands, add real alignment rituals.
- *Mastery*: "**If our top person disappeared for a month, what would break?**" Whatever you just thought of needs a playbook, a backup, and a teacher.

Visionary Builders don't micromanage; they architect. You're designing a culture where the right behavior is the easiest behavior, where the truth has a standing meeting, and where knowledge travels faster than problems. Do that, and your presence becomes a force multiplier, not a bottleneck.

Bottom line: *S.U.M.* scales your growth from personal to organizational. Change the system so collaboration wins. Create unity so direction holds. Share knowledge so capacity expands. Then run the loop again—faster, cleaner, with more people pulling in the same direction. That's how transformation stops depending on one leader and starts living in the DNA of the whole enterprise.

Don't just lead—build.

The Asset Navigator — *Scaling From Builder to Strategic Investor*

You've built something real. Now the question changes: can your capital work as hard as you did? **The Asset Navigator** extends the Circle of Growth beyond **S.U.M. (System, Unity, Mastery)** and turns your leadership instincts into an investing discipline. The aim is simple and serious: grow wealth, preserve it across generations, and deploy it for impact. This is the bridge from operator to owner; from doing the work to designing a portfolio that does the work.

11) **Vision, Values, Identity** — *Align the Why of Your Wealth*

Great investors begin where great leaders begin: with purpose. Define what your money is for—freedom, family stability, community projects, philanthropy—then let that vision filter every decision.

- *Write a Wealth Mission*: "My capital enables X for Y by Z."
- Name 3–5 core values (*e.g., integrity, innovation, service*) and refuse deals that violate them—no matter the upside.
- Install guardrails for your temperament. If you're cautious, codify downside limits. If you're hype-prone, require a cooling period and external review.

When markets get loud, your mission keeps you steady. When a shiny deal appears, your values say yes—or no— before your ego does.

12) **The Investor's Mindset** — *Patience, Discipline, Resilience*

You've been a builder; now you're an allocator. The skill shifts from making products to placing capital.

- Patience: let compounding work over years, not days.
- Discipline: invest by rule, not mood.
- Resilience: losses are tuition—extract the lesson and move.

Build fluency: read financials, understand ROI/IRR, cycles, risk/return by asset class. Start simple (*broad ETFs, REITs*) while you learn, and celebrate sticking to plan more than winning a trade. Confidence should come from skill, not luck.

13) **Strategy You Can Stick To** — *Your IPS*

Structure beats impulse. Draft a one-page Investment Policy Statement:

- Objectives: growth, income, preservation, impact— rank them.
- Horizons: short (0–3 yrs), medium (3–10), long (10+).
- Risk rules: position limits, drawdown thresholds, liquidity minimums.

- Target allocation across asset classes.
- Selection criteria: the checklist every investment must pass.
- Decision process: who reviews, cooling periods, dollar limits.
- Rebalancing cadence and contingency playbook for shocks.

A living IPS turns noise into non-events and keeps your capital pointed at your purpose.

14) **Unity Through Network & Mentors** — *Don't Go Alone*

Great investors compound relationships.

- Join peer circles (*angels, REIAs, operator forums*).
- Recruit mentors who've played the game you're entering.
- Assemble a light advisory bench: CPA, attorney, planner, specialist counsel.
- At home, run calm, age-appropriate family finance huddles so vision, values, and expectations stay aligned.

Give as much as you ask. Being useful makes opportunity boomerang back.

15) **Allocation & Diversification** — *Build the Engine*

Return is earned in selection; survival is earned in sizing.

Mix across: equities, fixed income, real estate (*direct, REITs, syndications*), private markets, alternatives, cash.

Diversify within each (*sector, style, geography, duration*). Keep liquidity for shocks and shots. Rebalance on schedule.

Simple rules that save fortunes:

- No single position > 5% (*private deals even smaller*).
- Always hold a cash cushion.
- Favor low-correlation pairings (*e.g., quality bonds with equities; real assets as inflation hedges*).

16) **Due Diligence & Risk** — *Protect the Downside*

Never invest blind.

- Understand the money machine: how returns are created, by whom, on what assumptions.
- Underwrite the people: track record, skin in the game, references.
- Model the numbers: revenue, margins, leverage, cash flow; for property—cap rates, DSCR, vacancy scenarios.
- Read the docs: fees, rights, exits, contingencies.

Mitigate with position sizing, insurance, sensible leverage, and pre-defined exit/stop rules. If the thesis breaks, you exit. Pride is not a strategy.

17) **Tax & Structure** — *Keep What You Earn*

It's not what you make; it's what you keep.

- Asset location: park tax-inefficient income (*bonds, REITs*) in tax-advantaged accounts; keep tax-

efficient equities in taxable; harvest losses when appropriate.
- Use the right entities (*LLCs for property/liability, trusts for estate aims, DAFs/foundations for giving*).
- Plan big moves (*business sales, 1031s, Roth conversions*) with a pro.
- Review annually—laws change, your plan should too.

18) **Mastery** — *Learn, Review, Adapt*

Schedule quarterly/annual reviews:

- Compare results to goals; rebalance; prune fees.
- Run post-mortems on wins and losses (*was it skill or luck?*).
- Scan for regime shifts (*rates, tech, regulation*) and adapt with reason, not reaction.
- Teach what you know—mentoring cements your own mastery.

- Curiosity keeps you current; humility keeps you solvent.

19) **Legacy** — *Design Impact That Outlives You*

Wealth becomes significance when it carries values forward.

- Clarify the legacy: family stability, community uplift, enduring institutions.
- Prepare heirs with education, participation, and clear governance.
- Use wills/trusts (*and, if needed, a simple "**family constitution**"*) to codify intent.
- Embed giving via DAFs or foundations; measure impact like you measure return.

Succession is a gift: to your family, your operators, and your causes.

20) **Grow Where You Are** — *Non-Linear, On Purpose*

Growth isn't a ladder—it's a loop. You'll cycle through these stages again, each pass with more wisdom. Follow genuine interest to sustain momentum, but don't skip foundations. Master the step you're in; let that mastery fund the next.

From Success to Significance

The Asset Navigator turns your leadership DNA into an investing operating system. Align the why, build the system, share the knowledge, and let disciplined capital express your values at scale. You're no longer just building companies; you're architecting a legacy—one that compounds in returns, relationships, and real-world good.

Conclusion

Light the Loop

Light the Loop – Field Guide

Welcome to the field guide section of **Light the Loop**. *Now that you've explored the ideas, it's time to* **run the loop** *for real. This is your hands-on playbook – clear steps, casual language, and encouraging tips to turn the Circle of Growth into daily practice. No lofty jargon or "poster values" here – just patterns that work. Whether you're a student leading a class project, an entrepreneur running a small business, or simply working on yourself, these pages will help you put character into action. Remember, leadership boils down to two things you control:* **who you are** *and* **what you do next**. *The Circle of Growth links those together in a simple, repeatable cycle. In other words, if you can run a loop, you can lead with intention – and prove it. Let's break down exactly how to do that.*

The Loop: Your New Leadership Rhythm

Think of the Circle of Growth as a **loop** *– a cycle you'll run over and over to translate inner values into outward results. Every time you run it, clarity turns into action, action turns into outcomes, and outcomes teach you how to improve next time. Picture a flywheel diagram here – each rotation building momentum from the last. (Imagine a circular "flywheel" graphic showing the seven steps feeding into each other.) The goal is to build steady, compounding progress, not one-off wins. Here's how to run the loop step by step:*

1. **Assess – Start with the truth.** *Take a clear-eyed look at where things stand before you make a plan. What's your real baseline? What are the actual facts, risks, and assumptions in front of you? Identify who's responsible for what from the start. No spin, no wishful thinking – just an honest assessment you can build on. Example: If you're a student team beginning a project, Assess by reviewing the assignment requirements, each member's skills, and any challenges or deadlines you know about. Everyone gets on the same page about reality.*

2. **Clarify – Define the goal and the plan.** *Now that you have the truth, decide where to go with it. What outcome are you aiming for? Break that down into crystal-clear targets, roles, and timing. In plain language, spell out what "success" looks like and who will do which part. Clarity beats chaos: when everyone knows what "done" means and why it matters, people can move with confidence. Example: For that class project, Clarify by setting a specific goal (e.g.* **"Score at least 90% on our presentation"**) *and assign tasks – who will research, who will design slides, who will present. Set deadlines for each task. This way, there's no confusion about what needs to happen.*

3. **Harness – Align resources and focus.** *Gather your people, time, and tools and point them toward the priority. Cut out the busywork or "nice-to-*

haves" that don't serve the goal. Limit how many things you tackle at once (no endless multitasking or massive to-do lists). The idea is to concentrate effort where it counts most right now. Example: A small business owner might Harness by scheduling all staff on the busy shift and ensuring they have the tools/training needed for one key initiative at a time. You stop juggling 10 projects and focus on finishing the one that will make the biggest impact this week. (Visual hint: imagine a checklist icon here, symbolizing how you might list and allocate key resources.)

4. **Innovate – Work smarter, not just harder.** Look for ways to improve the process and solve problems creatively. This is where you ask, "How can we do this better?" Maybe you try a new method, simplify a workflow, or introduce a tool – always aligning with your values and mission (no cutting corners on integrity). Small experiments are great here: test, learn, and iterate. Example: If a particular study method isn't working for your group, Innovate by trying a different approach – say, using flashcards or a mock quiz – to see if it yields better understanding. Or if you run a bakery and morning coffee service is slow, experiment with a new prep process or layout to speed things up. **Bold ideas, yes – but always true to your principles (no "innovation" that betrays trust).** (You might visualize this as a lightbulb or a quadrant diagram exploring new vs. old methods.)

5. **Empower – Share responsibility and grow others.** Don't micromanage – give people ownership of their work with the support to succeed. Set the vision or standards ("the what") but let your team have input on how to get there. Create an environment where it's safe to speak up, ask questions, and even fail and try again. Recognition and trust are key: celebrate wins and give credit, and widen access to information and tools so more people can contribute. Example: In a school club, Empower members by letting each person lead a part of the project they're passionate about, and make it safe for them to propose ideas. In a small business, this could mean training an employee to handle social media their own way within basic guidelines. You're effectively saying, "I trust you to run with this – I've got your back." When people feel ownership, they bring their best. (Picture a team icon or a hand-off graphic here, indicating delegated ownership.)

6. **Validate – Check the results and learn.** As you take action, constantly measure what actually happens against what you expected. In simple terms: **"Is it working? Prove it."** Define a few real outcomes or metrics that matter, and track them on a regular rhythm. Don't wait until it's too late – get feedback early and often. Let data or tangible evidence inform your next move, rather than hunches or wishful thinking. Example: If you're trying a new study method, look at quiz scores or recall ability to see if it's helping. In a

business, if you launched that new coffee prep process, check the morning sales numbers or customer wait times. Review these weekly or at the end of a project cycle. The point is not to judge or assign blame, but to learn. **Facts over ego:** maybe your idea wasn't as effective as hoped – that's okay, now you know to adjust. By validating, you turn "failure" into data for improvement.

7. **Execute – Deliver on the plan with discipline.** This is where you finish strong and fulfill the promise – the "do it" part. No almost-done work or abandoned projects; you ship the result to the defined standard of done. Stick to the quality bar you set and maintain any margins or limits (time, budget, etc.) you need to respect. Execution is about consistency and reliability – doing what you said you would do, the way you said you would do it. Example: For our student project, Execute by rehearsing and then giving the presentation on the due date, hitting all the points you planned. In business, Execute might mean completing the product launch on schedule, with all features working and marketing ready to go. It's not glamorous – it's just making sure the work actually gets across the finish line. In the end, **"done" is the metric that matters**. As we like to say: no slides, no excuses – **just results**.

That's one full loop! **Assess → Clarify → Harness → Innovate → Empower → Validate → Execute** – seven *moves that turn who you are into what you do. You can run this play on any project, with any team, in any season of life. And here's the magic: each pass through the loop makes the next one smoother. Every cycle tightens your aim, builds trust, and speeds up delivery. It's like practicing a sport or instrument – you build muscle memory. At first, you might need checklists or reminders for each step (pro tip: keep a simple* **checklist** *of the 7 Actions on your desk for focus). But soon, it becomes a habit.*

Run the loop on a regular cadence. *Think in weeks and quarters. For example, many leaders use a* **weekly rhythm** *to stay on track. (Imagine a simple "rhythm chart" of the week with slots for each step.) Every week, take a short pause – even 15-30 minutes – to ask:*

- **What mattered?** *(What did we accomplish or learn this week?)*

- **What shipped?** *(What did we actually deliver or finish?)*

- **What's blocked?** *(Where are we stuck or struggling?)*

- **What's next?** *(Based on that, what's the priority for next week?)*

This quick review (perhaps in a team huddle or personal journal) keeps you honest and the loop moving. Then, every quarter or so, step back for a bigger review: look at your key metrics and goals, celebrate wins, and adjust your game plan for the next quarter. Think of it as a seasonal tune-up for your loop.

One important note: **don't skip steps.** *Each action in the loop is there for a reason. If you skip* **Assess**, *you're flying blind. Skip* **Clarify**, *and people run in different directions. Neglect* **Harness**, *and resources get scattered and wasted. Ignore* **Innovate**, *and you'll stagnate. Fail to* **Empower**, *and your team's talent and honesty will dry up. Skip* **Validate**, *and you'll base decisions on guesswork. And if you don't* **Execute**, *well... nothing actually gets delivered. Running the full loop, in order, is how you compound small wins into big results.*

So, **run the play like a pro:** *start with truth, point the effort, align the muscle, improve the machine, unlock the humans, prove the progress, finish the work – then do it again. This is how strategy stops being something on paper and starts being something you actually live. Week by week, you'll find that your life and work tighten around what truly matters. Less wasted time, more intentional action. And when you run it with others, you'll notice something even cooler: a culture begins to form – one where truth is safe to tell, wins are shared, and everyone grows together.*

The 7 Traits: Who You Are

*At the heart of the Circle of Growth are **7 core traits** – the inner mindset or character qualities that fuel each part of the loop. Think of these as the "who you are" that powers "what you do." Leadership isn't just about tactics; it starts inside. The good news is, these traits aren't fixed personality traits – they're habits of character you can practice and strengthen. Here's a quick tour of each trait, why it matters, and how it shows up in real life:*

1. **Self-Awareness** – Know yourself to improve yourself. This trait is all about being honest with yourself: understanding your habits, your triggers, your strengths, and blind spots. When you're self-aware, you catch your ego or fears before they derail you. You see how your behavior impacts others, and you course-correct early. Example: A self-aware student might notice, "I tend to procrastinate when I'm anxious about an assignment," and then take action to break that pattern (like starting earlier or asking for help). In a team, a self-aware leader might admit, "I'm not great with details – I'll loop in someone who is," rather than pretend to know it all. This trait powers the **Assess** step, because you have to be truthful about where you stand before you can grow.

2. **Courage** – Choose candor and action over comfort. Courage isn't just bravery in big heroic

moments – it's the daily choice to face discomfort and tell the truth, even when it's awkward. This trait means you speak up about issues instead of hiding them, and you make the hard decisions when others might delay. It's also about **psychological courage**: creating an atmosphere where others feel safe to be honest. Example: A courageous team member will say "Guys, our plan isn't working – here's why," instead of staying silent to avoid conflict. Or as a leader, you might have that tough conversation with an underperforming employee sooner rather than later. Courage powers the **Clarify** step – it takes courage to set a bold goal and to have frank discussions about roles, expectations, and problems. If you practice courage daily (like giving honest feedback kindly, or asking a question everyone else is avoiding), you'll find small problems surface while they're still small – which is exactly what you want.

3. **Humility** – Stay teachable and team-focused. Humility means staying grounded and open-minded. It's recognizing that you don't have all the answers and that good ideas can come from anywhere. A humble leader listens more than they talk. They let better ideas rise – even if those ideas aren't their own. Humility isn't about thinking less of yourself; it's about thinking of yourself less – keeping the mission and team above your ego. Example: In daily life, humility might look like a student asking for feedback on an essay and truly

considering the critique, rather than getting defensive. In a business, a humble manager might invite the junior staff to share suggestions to improve a process – and actually implement a suggestion, giving credit where it's due. This trait fuels **Harness** *and* **Innovate** *– because to align people and resources well, and to improve the system, you must first listen and acknowledge that others might know a better way. Humility keeps the system smarter than any one person, so ideas flow and the whole group rises.*

4. **Integrity** *– Do the right thing, even when it's hard. Integrity is about honesty and consistency between your values and your actions. It's doing what's right when no one's watching, and upholding principles even when it costs you. If you promised something, you deliver. If something goes wrong, you don't cover it up – you address it. Integrity builds* **trust***, which is the currency of leadership. Example: An everyday integrity move could be a student admitting they made a mistake on a group project (rather than quietly letting the error slide), because fixing it is the right thing to do. Or in business, it might mean turning down a quick but unethical deal, or being transparent with customers about an issue. Integrity powers the* **Innovate** *step in the loop – that might sound odd at first, but think of it this way: when you seek to improve or change how you do things, integrity ensures you improve the right way. You're not cutting ethical corners for the sake of results. Also,*

innovation often means pushing into unknown territory; integrity keeps you anchored to your values so you don't lose trust in the process.

5. **Empathy** – *Lead with understanding of others. Empathy is recognizing and respecting people's feelings and perspectives. It means you remember that your team, customers, and partners are human beings, not just cogs or "resources." With empathy, you actively try to see things through others' eyes. This trait creates psychological safety – when people feel understood and valued, they're more willing to take ownership and risks. Example: A teacher leading a class project shows empathy by checking in with a student who seems frustrated to understand what's going on, rather than just scolding them for slacking. In a company, an empathetic manager might adjust a deadline when they realize their team is burning out, or offer flexibility to someone dealing with personal challenges. Empathy fuels* **Empower** – *because to truly empower others, you have to trust them and care about their growth. Leading with empathy means you're not just managing tasks; you're mentoring people. It turns a group of individuals into a team that has each other's backs.*

6. **Learning (Growth Mindset)** – *Stay adaptable and curious. The trait of Learning is about being teachable and hungry to improve. It's acknowledging you don't know it all and that there's always room to grow. When you have a*

learning mindset, setbacks don't crush you – they instruct you. You seek feedback, read, ask questions, and experiment. Every experience becomes a chance to get better rather than proof of failure. Example: A student with a learning mindset, upon getting a low score, will ask "What can I do differently next time?" instead of "I guess I'm just bad at this." In a business context, a learning-focused leader might run a retrospective after a project – even a successful one – to ask, "What can we learn from this? What could we do better?" This trait is the engine for **Validate** *– because learning requires looking at the evidence and adjusting. If you're not willing to learn, you won't truly validate (you'd either ignore the data or refuse to change). Leaders who embody learning turn mistakes into momentum and make their teams places where continuous improvement is the norm.*

7. **Execution (Discipline)** – *Finish what you start. Execution as a trait means you have the habit of following through with consistency. It's the gritty discipline to actually do the work, day in and day out, especially when it's not easy or fun. Leaders with this trait don't just start projects – they complete them and deliver results. They also instill discipline in their teams: clear standards, routines, and accountability. Execution isn't about rushing; it's about reliability. Example: A disciplined student sets a schedule and sticks to it – say, "I write 500 words every morning at 8am" – and so the paper gets finished well before the deadline (instead of a last-minute panic). In a workplace, a leader with execution discipline will establish, for instance, a regular Tuesday check-in meeting and never miss it, or will enforce a "definition of done" for tasks so nothing falls through the cracks. This trait propels the **Execute** step (naturally) – it's what turns plans into tangible outcomes. When you have a culture of execution, things get done and people can trust that promises made will be kept.*

Take a moment to reflect: which of these traits comes naturally to you? Which one might be a growth area? The beauty of the Circle of Growth is that it links **character to action**. If you find a certain action step consistently hard, strengthening the corresponding trait will help. For example, if **Clarify** (setting clear goals) is tough, focus on practicing **Courage** – have those uncomfortable clarifying conversations, say the specifics you usually shy *away from. Over time, who you are (your traits) and what you do (your actions) start reinforcing each other. Your inner game fuels your outer game, and vice versa.* **Character becomes execution.**

One more tip: these traits aren't just solo virtues; they affect your whole team or environment. When you model these traits, others catch on. For instance, your personal integrity makes it likelier that your team will be transparent and ethical. Your courage in admitting a mistake makes it safer for others to do the same. In that way, who you are scales – it creates a ripple effect. We'll talk more about scaling in the S.U.M. section, but keep in mind: **leadership is caught as much as it's taught.** *Live the traits, and you set a powerful example.*

The 7 Actions: What You Do

If traits are the mindset, **Actions** *are the moves. These 7 Actions are the concrete steps in the loop – the "what you do" part of leadership. We've already gone through them as the steps of the Loop, but let's summarize them here with a bit more actionable flavor for quick reference (each action pairs with the trait we just discussed):*

1. **Assess** – *Tell the truth (start with reality). This is your* **fact-finding and grounding** *step. Before you charge ahead, pause to ask: Where are we really? Gather data, scan the environment, identify risks and assumptions, and assign initial owners for tasks. The motto here is "No truth, no progress." A leader who Assesses well will, for example, begin a new quarter by reviewing last quarter's results*

and lessons, or a student will start an assignment by reading the rubric and feedback on past assignments. **Tool tip:** Consider using a simple checklist of questions to guide Assess (e.g. "What's our baseline metric? Biggest risk? Who needs to be involved?"). This ensures you're not wearing rose-colored glasses. Trait link: Needs **Self-Awareness and honesty.**

2. **Clarify** – Get specific about success. Once you know where you are, decide where to go and how to get there. Clarify means **setting clear goals, roles, and plans** in plain language. No vague aspirations – pin down the target (what outcome you want), the timeframe, the priorities, and who is accountable for what. Think of it as drawing the map and assigning seats in the car. A team that clarifies well will come out of a meeting knowing exactly who will do **Which Thing** by **When** (and why it matters). When you clarify, you remove ambiguity: everyone should know what "done" looks like. Trait link: Runs on **Courage** (to define bold goals and speak unspoken expectations).

3. **Harness** – Align and focus the resources. Now, make sure all your horses are pulling the wagon in the same direction. Harness is about **coordination and focus**. It involves allocating people to tasks matching their strengths, scheduling time realistically, and prepping tools or budget needed for execution. Crucially, it also means **saying no** to distractions: if something

isn't a priority, park it or cut it. To harness effectively, you might limit work-in-progress (e.g. "We'll tackle only these two features this week, nothing else") and streamline communication (e.g. one channel for project updates). The result: less thrash, more flow. Trait link: Requires **Humility** and team-orientation – you have to trust others and organize efforts beyond just yourself.

4. **Innovate** – Improve the process or idea. This action is about **working smarter**. Innovate asks: How can we do this better, or get better results? Maybe you need a creative solution to a problem, or a new method entirely. It could be a small tweak (changing the order of tasks) or a big change (pivoting your approach), but it should be grounded in learning and aligned with your values. Importantly, innovating isn't "change for change's sake" – it's purposeful. For example, a team might run a mini-experiment: "Let's try a daily 5-minute stand-up meeting to see if it clears roadblocks faster." If it works, great, you've upgraded your process. If not, no harm – you learned something. Embrace a bit of curiosity here. Trait link: Needs **Integrity** (so your innovations solve problems without compromising principles) and a dash of courage too.

5. **Empower** – Let others lead and grow. This step is about **delegating and enabling**. After you've aligned the plan and maybe improved it, don't try to do everything yourself – multiply your impact

through others. Empower means you entrust others with meaningful responsibilities, give them authority along with guidance (guardrails), and then step back and let them work. It also means acknowledging and celebrating their contributions, so they feel ownership. Practically, to empower you might say, "Alex, you're in charge of testing this feature – let me know what you need," and then truly let Alex run with it, intervening only if necessary. Create forums where even quiet team members can voice ideas. And make sure credit and wins are shared, not hogged. When people feel empowered, they take initiative and the whole project benefits from more brainpower and heart. Trait link: Runs on **Empathy** *(to understand and trust your people's needs and potential).*

6. **Validate** – *Verify progress with evidence. Here you shift into a learning and measurement mode:* **are we actually making progress?** *To validate, set up a few clear metrics or indicators at the start (during Clarify) and check them regularly. Examples: test scores, customer sign-ups, bug counts, budget vs. actual spend – whatever "success" means for your goal. Then create a rhythm (say, every Friday or end of sprint) to review these. Ask "What does the data say? What can it teach us?" Importantly, validating includes reviewing – taking time to reflect on what's working or not. You might run a retrospective meeting, or simply do a personal journal entry:*

"This week's results: what do they tell me?" And if the evidence shows a gap, you **adapt** – tweak the plan, try a new tactic, or sometimes reconsider the goal. The key habit here is not to shy away from feedback. Trait link: Needs **Learning** mindset – curiosity and humility to accept reality and adjust.

7. **Execute** – Get it done, the right way. This is the **follow-through** step where you cross the finish line. To execute means to deliver your work completely and correctly, meeting the definition of done you set. It's about consistency – doing what you promised every time. It might involve final quality checks, adhering to standards, and ensuring the outcome is usable/ready. Execution often comes down to good habits: using checklists so nothing is missed (pilots and surgeons do this!), time-blocking to focus on deep work, and maintaining personal and team accountability. Example: Execution for a writer might be their daily word-count goal; for a sales team, it might be making those 10 client calls every single day regardless of mood. And if an obstacle arises, executors find a way around it or a way to still deliver something of value. Trait link: Relies on **Execution (Discipline)** trait – self-control and responsibility.

These 7 Actions form a **repeatable workflow** you can apply to any project or goal. In fact, you might recognize them as common-sense steps – many people do some of these naturally. The power of the Circle of Growth is in doing all seven intentionally and on a steady rhythm. It's a closed loop: as soon as you Execute, you start Assessing the next cycle. Over time, you'll find this approach crowds out procrastination and "random busyness." Instead of wondering what to do next, you have a built-in process: finish, assess, clarify, and go again. It turns leadership into an ongoing practice rather than a one-time push.

To make these actions even more concrete, consider a quick real-life scenario of running the loop:

> **Example – Running the Loop in a Small Business:** Jaime runs a local bakery and wants to boost morning sales. She starts by **Assessing** the current situation – reviewing sales data and customer feedback (truth: the line is slow and customers often skip coffee). She **Clarifies** the goal: "Increase morning coffee sales by 20% in the next 8 weeks," and outlines a plan with her team (introduce a new quick-service coffee station, target = 50 more cups a day, assign Ana to oversee it, trial it for 2 months). Next, they **Harness** resources – reassign one staff member to handle just coffee during the rush, invest in a faster coffee machine, and rearrange the counter for efficiency (all efforts focused on the one goal). They **Innovate** by devising a simple pre-order system using text messages to cut wait time, trying it out for a week to see if it helps. Jaime **Empowers** Ana to adjust the process

as needed and encourages the whole team to suggest improvements (and she makes sure to praise the team at weekly meetings for every little win, like a faster serve time). They **Validate** *progress by tracking daily coffee sales and customer wait times each week, discussing results every Friday. They learn that the pre-order system is catching on, but also discover via feedback that the new machine's coffee taste needs tweaking – so they adjust the brew. Finally, they* **Execute** *by sticking to the plan every morning without fail – opening the coffee station on time, using the new process, and serving each cup with quality. At the 8-week mark, sales are up 25%. They then roll into the next cycle: Assess what worked (and what didn't) in this experiment, then Clarify the next goal (maybe boosting lunchtime bakery sales next). In this way, Jaime's bakery keeps improving in steady, manageable loops, rather than chaotic leaps.*

By now, you might be thinking: This sounds like a lot! Don't worry. It feels natural once you get going, and you're likely doing bits of it already. The key is to be deliberate and consistent. Eventually, running the loop becomes second nature – a leadership habit. Also, remember you're not alone in this: involve your team or peers. Share the loop concept with them. Use the same language of Assess, Clarify, etc., in meetings. It creates a shared playbook, so everyone knows what it means, for example, when you say "Let's validate that assumption" or "We need to harness our efforts around this priority."

The 7 Ps: Where It Applies (Focus Areas)

You've got the how (Actions) and the who (Traits). Now let's talk about the where. The **7 Ps** are seven focus areas or domains of work where you apply the loop. They ensure you're covering all the bases of whatever you're leading. Think of the 7 Ps as a checklist of "places to look" or levers to adjust when running the loop. When you cycle through Assess → Execute, you'll touch on each of these areas so nothing important slips through the cracks:

1. **Purpose** – Why you're doing the work. Every project or endeavor should start with this question: **What's the purpose?** This P is about vision, direction, and success criteria. It's the North Star that guides all other decisions. In practice, focusing on Purpose means clearly defining the "why" and the endstate. If you're a student group, Purpose might be "to create an app that helps our classmates manage homework (because we want to reduce stress)." In a business, Purpose could be "to provide affordable healthy meals in our community." Keeping Purpose front and center helps align everyone's effort and fuels motivation – especially when things get tough. (Visual cue: a target or flag icon for purpose.) When running the loop, **Assess** and **Clarify** naturally tie into Purpose – you assess the current situation in light of your purpose, and you clarify goals that serve

that purpose. A quick gut-check: if an activity doesn't serve the Purpose, why are you doing it?

2. **People** – Who's involved and how they work together. This area covers your team, stakeholders, and the human element of execution. It's about talent, trust, communication, and collaboration. Questions to ask: Do we have the right people in the right roles? Does everyone understand their role and feel accountable? Is trust high or do we need to address conflicts? Whether it's a group project, a nonprofit, or a company department, **People** make or break the effort. In practice, focusing on People might mean investing time in team-building, giving feedback, resolving a tension between two team members, or ensuring roles are clearly defined (maybe via a RACI chart or just a frank conversation). When running the loop, the **Clarify** and **Empower** actions often address People: you clarify roles and priorities with courage, and you empower folks with empathy and trust. Remember, no one wins solo. If People are set up well – clear, capable, and motivated – everything else moves faster. If People issues are ignored, even the best plans stall.

3. **Product** – What value you're creating. "Product" here means the outcome or thing you are delivering, not necessarily a physical product. It could be a service, a project deliverable, an event – whatever is the value you provide to your "customers" (which might be users, clients, your

community, or your teacher). Focusing on Product means asking: Are we actually solving the problem or meeting the need we set out to? Is our output high quality and useful? It's easy to get caught up in tasks and forget to evaluate if the result is any good. In a software project, Product focus means user-testing to ensure the app is actually helpful. In a school context, it means checking if your science project actually works and demonstrates the concept, not just if it meets the format guidelines. **Innovate** and **Validate** actions often come into play here – you might innovate to make the product better (e.g. refine a feature based on feedback), and validate by measuring how well the product is performing (e.g. are users using it? Did the audience learn something from our presentation?). A common mantra: "Make something people want." Always loop back to, are we delivering real value?

4. **Process** – How the work flows. Process is all about the **systems and procedures** you use to do the work. It asks: Are our methods effective and efficient? Do we have the right routines and tools? Where are things getting stuck? In teams, good processes might include regular check-ins, a shared to-do board, documented steps for key tasks, etc. In personal productivity, it could be your daily schedule or task management method. Paying attention to Process means you prefer **consistent, reliable flow over ad-hoc heroics**. For example, rather than relying on a last-minute

crunch (heroics) every time, you build a process that avoids the crunch – like a content calendar for marketing posts instead of scrambling for ideas every day. In our loop, the **Harness** *and* **Execute** *steps often involve Process – harnessing includes setting up the workflow, and execute benefits from a clear process (like a checklist or quality control routine). Tip: If something in your project felt chaotic or painful (miscommunications, delays, quality issues), look at Process – how can you simplify or improve the steps to prevent that pain next time? Process improvements are usually "unsexy" things like templates, schedules, or backup plans, but they greatly increase your capacity.*

5. **Principles** *– The values and guidelines that shape decisions. Principles are the bedrock values or non-negotiables that guide how you operate. This P ensures that in pursuing results, you don't abandon the values that matter (and that you maintain culture). Essentially, are we doing this the right way, ethically and aligned with our values? Also, are our team norms and rules encouraging the right behaviors? For instance, a principle might be "We treat each other with respect, even when we disagree," or "Safety first," or "Integrity in all customer communications." When running the loop,* **Empower** *and* **Innovate** *both should be influenced by Principles – you empower within value-driven guardrails, and you innovate in ways consistent with your mission and ethics (no*

cheating to get a better metric). A practical way to apply Principles is to establish a short list of team principles at the start of a project (e.g. "We will be candid and kind"; "We value sustainability in our materials"; "No shortcuts that sacrifice quality"). Then when tough decisions come, you filter options through these principles. Over time, principles become part of the culture – everyone knows "this is how we do things here." It speeds up decision-making and keeps trust high, because people know there's integrity between the actions.

6. **Performance** – *Measures of progress and results. Performance is about* **tracking outcomes** *– the metrics, KPIs, or benchmarks that tell you how you're doing. It's closely tied to the Validate action, obviously. Focusing on Performance means you define what success looks like in measurable terms ("increase sales by 20%," "get an A on the project," "reduce processing time to 2 days") and then you regularly check those measures. It's also about cadence: establishing regular reviews (weekly, monthly, quarterly) to gauge performance. One key aspect of Performance is distinguishing between leading indicators (things that predict future success, like number of study hours per week might predict exam scores) and lagging indicators (the end results, like the exam score itself). Good leaders track a few of both. By paying attention to Performance, you avoid the trap of just "being*

busy" and instead make sure you're productive. In meetings you might hear, "Let's look at the numbers" – that's Performance focus. But it's not just numbers; it's learning from those numbers. As the loop philosophy says, adapt without drama when the data speaks. Keep performance metrics limited to what truly matters, so you don't drown in data. And celebrate progress you see! That fuels motivation for the next loop.

7. **Profit** – *Sustainable outcomes you can reinvest. Profit represents* **the payoff and how it's reinvested**. *In a business, yes, it literally means financial profit – money earned after expenses. But more broadly, think of Profit as the results that keep your mission sustainable. This could be money, but it could also be things like user satisfaction, impact on the community, personal energy or morale gains, knowledge gained, etc. The key is that you treat those results as fuel for the next cycle. For example, a nonprofit's "profit" might be the increased number of people helped; they then reinvest that social capital or fundraising into expanding their programs. On a personal level, "profit" might be the new free time you earned by improving efficiency, which you then reinvest into learning a new skill. Focusing on Profit ensures you close the loop by asking: Did we get the outcome we wanted? How can we use this success (or failure) to fund future growth? In practice, for a business it might mean allocating a portion of earnings to R&D or team bonuses (so success breeds more*

success), or for a student who aced an exam, it could mean leveraging that confidence into tackling a harder class next semester. Profit in our loop aligns with **Execute** *– it's the end result of execution – and then connects back to Purpose by reinvesting in what's next. It reminds us that growth should be sustainable; each win should strengthen your foundation, not just be a one-time high. Stewardship is a good word here: treat your results as resources to take care of and deploy wisely for future gain.*

These 7 Ps give our loop context. Whenever you're problem-solving or planning, you can mentally run down this list to diagnose issues or find opportunities:

- *Are we clear on* **Purpose**? *(Or are we drifting without direction?)*

- *Do we have the right* **People** *and are they supported?*

- *Is our* **Product**/*outcome truly solving the need?*

- *How's our* **Process** *– smooth or clunky?*

- *Are we honoring our* **Principles** *along the way?*

- *What's our* **Performance** *telling us – any signals we need to heed?*

- And are we building **Profit** (sustainable gains) or are we burning out?

*The 7 Ps map closely to the 7 Actions: each action tends to "live" in one of these domains. For example, when you Assess, you're mainly addressing Purpose (finding the "why/where are we" baseline). Clarify lives in People (aligning team on roles and direction). Harness deals with Product and Process (focusing resources on delivering value efficiently). Innovate often touches Process and Principles (finding better ways that align with values). Empower is big on People and Principles (trust and values in action). Validate ties to Performance (measuring results), and Execute hits Profit (delivering outcomes to reinvest). You don't need to memorize those pairings – the cheat sheet at the end will lay it out – but as you gain experience, you'll start to see how trait → action → P connects in a tight logic. It's a **holistic system**: who you are (Traits) drives what you do (Actions) in all the areas that matter (Ps).*

By checking all 7 Ps, you avoid common leadership blind spots. For instance, some very visionary people focus a lot on Purpose and Product but might neglect Process or Performance (so they have great ideas but poor execution or no measurement). Others might hammer on Performance and Profit and forget Purpose or Principles (leading to a soulless or unethical grind). The Circle of Growth forces you to balance these and keep the whole picture in view. Over time, you'll probably identify your strongest Ps and your weakest – and you can deliberately shore up the weak spots. The result is you become a more rounded leader who can handle both the **big picture and the details**, the **people side and the numbers side**.

(If you were to diagram this, imagine a wheel or pie divided into 7 segments labeled Purpose, People, Product, etc. – you could even self-assess how you're doing in each segment for a visual snapshot of your leadership balance.)

S.U.M.: Scaling Up (System, Unity, Mastery)

By now you've seen how the Circle of Growth loop ties together **Traits, Actions, and Ps** for an individual or a single team. But what happens when you want to spread this way of working beyond just you or your immediate circle? That's where **S.U.M.** comes in. S.U.M. stands for **System, Unity, Mastery** – three factors that **scale your personal growth into organizational culture**. In short, S.U.M. is how leadership moves from being about just you to being about everyone around you.

Think of S.U.M. as the next phase of the loop – some have even called it stages 8, 9, and 10 of the Circle (after the 7 Actions). It ensures that the progress you've made doesn't vanish when you step away. Here's the breakdown:

- **System** – Build structures that support the loop. This means embedding the values and behaviors of the Circle into the formal systems of your team or organization. For example, change the reward and incentive systems so that teamwork and truth-telling are encouraged (and not punished). Update processes or policies to reflect the loop: maybe your *company's performance reviews now include how well people practice the 7 Actions; or you create a template for project planning that follows Assess → Execute. System is about institutionalizing what works so it continues regardless of who's in charge. Daily life example: If you're the captain of a school club, a "system" could be a standard meeting agenda that always starts with an Assess (truth-sharing) segment and ends with Validate (action items review). Or as a family, a system might be a weekly family meeting where everyone shares and plans together. By making it a routine or policy, the practice becomes part of the group's DNA.* **Outcome:** *The environment nudges everyone to run the loop; it's not just driven by your personal willpower. (In an icon form, System might be represented by gears or infrastructure – the machinery that keeps things running.)*

- ***Unity*** *– Create team rhythms and alignment. Unity is about building a culture of* ***togetherness and shared direction****. It's making sure everyone is on the same page and moving in sync. In practice, Unity can mean regular all-hands meetings where the vision and progress are communicated openly (so everyone knows the Purpose and how their work ties in). It can mean cross-functional projects that break silos – people from different teams actually working together and understanding each other's goals. It definitely means establishing a common "language" of growth – for instance, if everyone in your company* *knows what "run the loop" or "validate this" means, you have unity in approach. Unity also involves rituals or traditions that build trust and camaraderie (anything from weekly shout-outs for courage and integrity, to team lunches that humanize relationships). The goal:* **the whole team or organization develops a shared heartbeat.** *When Unity is strong, you don't get departments undercutting each other or individuals drifting off with conflicting agendas – you get one team, one fight. Example: A small business might implement a quick daily stand-up for all staff – 5 minutes each morning, everyone says what they're focusing on (Assess/Clarify for the day) and any help needed. This creates alignment and catches issues early, fostering unity.* **Outcome:** *People feel "we're all in this together," which boosts trust and makes the loop run smoother at scale. (You can imagine a unity icon as a group of people in a circle or hands stacked together.)*

- **Mastery** *– Share knowledge and elevate capacity. Mastery at scale means developing people so that knowledge and skills are widely shared, not bottled up in a few experts. It's about* **teaching and cross-training***, creating a learning organization. In a team with Mastery, when someone learns a better way to do something, they document it or teach others. Mentorship is common. There's an emphasis on continuous professional development – workshops, book clubs, training sessions – so that* *everyone keeps leveling up. Crucially, Mastery fights the "hero syndrome" – where one person is the only one who can do X. Instead, it ensures redundancy and resilience: if one team member leaves or is out, others can cover because the know-how is shared. Example: On a personal level, if you've mastered the Circle of Growth, you might mentor a friend or colleague in it (thus spreading the skill). In a company, Mastery might look like an internal wiki or playbook where team members contribute tips and SOPs for various tasks, or pairing up colleagues to learn each other's roles. It could also involve inviting guest speakers or visiting other teams to learn their best practices.* **Outcome:** *The organization or community keeps getting smarter and more capable, beyond the abilities of any single person. Problems become easier to solve because somewhere, someone has insight and they're willing and able to share it. "No one person is a bottleneck" is the ideal. (Icon idea: an open book or lightbulb network, symbolizing shared knowledge.)*

When you put **System** + **Unity** + **Mastery** together, you create a self-sustaining growth culture. In such a culture, running the loop isn't just a personal habit you're driving – it becomes the way we do things around here. People hold each other accountable to it, even when you (the leader) are not in the room. That's a huge win: it means your leadership has scaled from a personality to a *platform. Or said differently, your influence is now baked into the system.*

Let's illustrate S.U.M. with a quick story:

> **Example – S.U.M. in action (Team Scenario):** *Imagine you manage a customer support team that you've trained in the Circle of Growth. Initially, you personally drive the loop – you encourage team members to Assess issues honestly, Clarify their daily goals, etc. As time goes on, you implement* **System** *by updating the helpdesk software to require an Assess step (techs must fill in "what is the root cause?" before escalating) and a Validate step (checking if the customer's issue was truly resolved, via a follow-up survey). You also tie part of performance reviews to how well team members improve their metrics (rewarding learning and adaptation, not just raw numbers). You foster* **Unity** *by holding a weekly support huddle where you share one customer success story and one lesson learned (so everyone learns together), and maybe even rotate team leads so everyone gets a taste of leadership. There's a shared scoreboard visible in the office showing team performance (transparency). For* **Mastery***, you set up a buddy system: experienced reps coach newer ones on tricky cases, and you encourage everyone to document any new workaround they discover in a "Support Playbook" wiki.*

Over a year, you notice you no longer need to remind folks to run the loop – they're doing it themselves. New hires quickly get up to speed because the training (thanks to Mastery) is robust. Trust and alignment are high; when a big issue hits, the team rallies instead of finger-pointing (Unity!). And the support metrics (like response time, customer satisfaction) keep improving because the System keeps everyone focused on what matters. In short, the culture now embodies continuous improvement – you've multiplied your leadership impact.

On a smaller scale, think about a **school project group** that decides to adopt these ideas. They might create a **System** by using a shared online checklist template for all projects (with sections for Assess, Clarify, etc.), ensure **Unity** by agreeing on a weekly meeting and open communication norms, and pursue **Mastery** by having each member teach something they're good at to the rest (one is great at research, another at design, etc., so everyone learns a bit of each). The result: even after the leader of the group graduates, the younger members carry on the same effective practices, and the club or team continues to thrive. That's S.U.M. at work.

To summarize S.U.M.:

- **System** – Change the environment and rewards so that running the loop is reinforced on a larger scale (team/organization). Structure and incentives support teamwork and continuous improvement.

- **Unity** – Create shared rhythms and alignment so that everyone is pulling in the same direction and feels part of a cohesive whole. Communication is open and frequent; the vision is collective.

- **Mastery** – Spread knowledge and skills so that growth isn't isolated. Everyone gets better, and best practices are common knowledge. The culture becomes one of teaching and learning.

When these three are in place, you've effectively **scaled the Circle of Growth from "me" to "we."** You'll know you've succeeded when the team continues to excel even without constant prodding. As one part of the book put it, S.U.M. is how your leadership "stops being a personality and becomes a platform" – meaning it's not about one charismatic or driven individual, but about a durable system others can plug into and thrive. It's how a team becomes an engine and a company becomes a cause.

One more extension beyond S.U.M. (for future thinking): once you have System, Unity, Mastery in an organization, you set the stage for legacy – the impact that outlives you, because the culture keeps compounding progress. But that's another chapter. For now, focus on getting S, U, and M working wherever you lead, even if it's just a small team or community group. It will multiply your efforts tremendously.

Circle of Growth Cheat Sheet (One-Page Blueprint)

*Finally, here's a one-page **cheat sheet** to summarize the entire Circle of Growth system. Use this as a quick reference or a checklist. You can snapshot it, print it, tape it to your wall, share it with your team – whatever keeps you looping!*

- **The Loop (Continuous Cycle):**

    1. **Assess** – Truth first. Get a real baseline: current state, risks, and who's responsible.

    2. **Clarify** – Name it. Define clear goals, outcomes, and roles. Everyone should know what "done" looks like.

    3. **Harness** – Focus up. Align people, time, and tools on one priority. Cut distractions and limit WIP (work-in-progress).

    4. **Innovate** – Improve it. Find a smarter way: new ideas, better process, small experiments. Keep it values-aligned (no compromising integrity).

    5. **Empower** – Share it. Delegate with trust and guardrails. Encourage input, recognize contributions, build ownership.

6. **Validate** – Check it. Measure real outcomes and review on a rhythm. Use data and feedback to adjust course.

7. **Execute** – Complete it. Deliver to "definition of done" with discipline. No half-finishes – consistency and quality are key. (Then go back to **1 – Assess** for the next loop! Each cycle = new insight + improvement.)

- **The 7 Traits (Who You Are – Inner Game):**
  Self-Awareness (see yourself honestly) – fuels Assess.
  Courage (face fears & speak truth) – fuels Clarify.
  Humility (stay teachable & team-first) – fuels Harness (and Innovate).
  Integrity (act by values, trustworthiness) – fuels Innovate (and all steps).
  Empathy (understand others) – fuels Empower.
  Learning (adapt and grow from input) – fuels Validate.
  Execution (discipline to follow through) – fuels Execute.
  Develop these traits daily – they are the mindset that powers the loop.

- **The 7 Ps (Where It Happens – Focus Areas):**
  Purpose – Direction & "Why" (start with this).
  People – Team & Roles (talent, trust, collaboration).
  Product – Value Output (the problem you're

solving or solution you deliver).
Process – How Work Flows (systems, steps, efficiency).
Principles – Values & Guidelines (ethics, culture, "how we do things").
Performance – Results & Metrics (evidence of progress, KPIs).
Profit – Sustainable Outcomes (resources to reinvest: money, impact, etc.).
Use these as a checklist in planning and retrospectives. E.g., "Are we clear on Purpose? Any People issues? What do metrics say?"

- **S.U.M. (Scaling Up Culture):**
System – Make it structural. Integrate the loop into systems & incentives (so teamwork and truth-telling are rewarded).
Unity – Make it shared. Build common rhythms, language, and trust so the group moves as one.
Mastery – Make it learned. Spread knowledge, train others, and develop skills at all levels (no one is a single point of failure).
This is how your personal growth system becomes a team or organizational culture – the loop goes viral (in a good way).

How to use this cheat sheet: Whenever you feel stuck or off-track, scan these bullets. For instance, if progress stalled, check the Action steps: Did you skip one? Or look at the Ps: maybe there's a People issue or unclear Purpose holding you back. Use S.U.M. pointers if you're trying to *influence at a larger scale. This blueprint is meant to remind you of the essentials at a glance.*

You've got everything you need to **run the loop**. *The Circle of Growth is now in your hands – a simple, flexible operating system for continuous improvement. Start with one small cycle: pick a project or goal that matters this week and go through the steps. Anyone can do this. Share it with your friends, your team, or your study group. Hold each other accountable and compare notes.*

In the end, remember the big picture: Purpose is the point. Intent is the engine. Systems make it repeatable. You have the purpose (your why), you set the intent (your next action), and now you have the system (the loop) to turn it into results, again and again. So light that loop – run it, learn, and go again. **Loop, lead, and watch growth compound.** *Every week, every quarter, every season of your life. You've got this!*

References & Bibliography

Thinkers, Operators, and Frameworks That Sharpened the Circle

- **Robert T. Kiyosaki – *Rich Dad Poor Dad* (1997):** Kiyosaki's bestselling personal finance classic challenged conventional money beliefs and introduced a mindset shift toward seeing money as a tool. It differentiated between assets that generate income and liabilities that drain resources, stressing that true wealth comes from acquiring income-producing assets rather than working endlessly for a paycheck. The book's emphasis on financial literacy and the *prosperity mindset* – teaching readers to "have money work for them" through investing and entrepreneurship – directly influenced the *Circle of Growth*'s focus on building assets, passive income, and an abundance mentality. By demystifying complex concepts (like cash flow, debt, and investing) for a broad audience, *Rich Dad Poor Dad* provided foundational lessons on discipline and informed risk-taking that sharpened the author's framework for wealth accumulation.

- **Stephen R. Covey – *The 7 Habits of Highly Effective People* (1989):** Covey's work introduced a principle-centered paradigm for personal effectiveness and leadership. It lays out seven enduring habits (from *Be Proactive* to *Sharpen the Saw*) that foster character development and *self-leadership*, rather than quick-fix personality tricks. Covey emphasizes internal change first: nurturing integrity, vision ("Begin with the end in mind"), time prioritization ("Put first things first"), win-win thinking, empathetic communication, synergy, and continuous improvement. This focus on aligning one's actions with core principles and progressing from **private victories** (independence) to **public victories** (interdependence) has deeply informed The Circle of Growth's emphasis on mindset and habit formation. By highlighting proactive responsibility, goal-setting guided by values, and collaborative success, Covey's framework helped shape the Circle's guidance on personal growth, productivity, and effective leadership.

- **Gino Wickman – *Traction: Get a Grip on Your Business* (2007):** In *Traction*, Wickman presents the **Entrepreneurial Operating System (EOS)** – a comprehensive, practical framework for running and scaling a business. This system outlines six key components of organizational success (Vision,

People, Data, Issues, Process, and Traction) and provides tools to strengthen each area. Wickman's approach instills discipline through clear vision-setting, the use of measurable metrics (scorecards and KPIs), and rigorous execution via "rocks" (90-day priorities) and meeting rhythms. *Traction's* influence on The Circle of Growth is evident in the framework's structural approach to growth: insisting on clarity of purpose, the right team roles, data-driven decision-making, and systematic problem-solving. By advocating *focus* and accountability at every level, EOS reinforced the author's belief in operating with a blueprint – ensuring that personal and professional growth efforts gain real *traction* through consistent execution toward one's vision.

- **Robert Greene – *The 48 Laws of Power* (1998):** Greene's influential treatise on strategy and human nature provides 48 timeless principles for understanding power dynamics in business and life. It distills lessons from history's power players, offering strategies to build influence, guard against manipulation, and exercise leadership shrewdly. Though controversial for its amoral tone, the book serves as a *practical guide* to the realities of competition and influence — "for anyone who wants power, observes power, or wants to arm themselves against power". Key themes like the importance of reputation management, strategic thinking, and emotional control have informed The Circle of Growth's nuance in dealing with real-world challenges. By acknowledging these laws (e.g. Law 5: "So Much Depends on Reputation" or Law 15: "Crush Your Enemy Totally"), the author's system emphasizes ethical leadership and situational awareness. *The 48 Laws of Power* sharpened the Circle's approach to *strategic leadership*, highlighting the balance between principled conduct and the savvy needed to navigate organizational politics and negotiations.

- **Warren Buffett** – Often regarded as one of the greatest investors of all time, Buffett embodies principles of *long-term value investing* and disciplined capital allocation. He follows Benjamin Graham's school of investing by seeking companies with strong fundamentals that trade below their intrinsic value. Buffett famously looks at businesses as whole entities rather than stock-price tickers, prioritizing high-quality companies with durable economic advantages ("moats") and competent management. His approach — buy-and-hold investing in assets you understand, focusing on fundamentals over market fads — has profoundly influenced The Circle of Growth's investment philosophy. Buffett's insistence on patience, frugality, and rational decision-making under uncertainty instills in the Circle a respect for evidence-based strategies and prudent risk management. His success illustrates how *sound judgment* and a long-term horizon can unlock compounding wealth, guiding readers to allocate capital wisely and think like owners rather than speculators.

- **Peter F. Drucker** – Known as the "father of modern management," Drucker pioneered many concepts that underpin effective leadership and organizational strategy. He introduced **Management by Objectives (MBO)** – the practice of setting clear, measurable goals throughout an organization – and coined the term "knowledge workers," foreseeing the rise of human intellect as the key resource in the 21st century. Drucker's philosophy centers on clarity of mission, decentralization, and empowering individuals, encapsulated by his famous axiom, *"What gets measured gets managed."* His holistic, systems-thinking view of organizations (BusinessWeek noted, *"What John Maynard Keynes is to economics or W. Edwards Deming to quality, Drucker is to management"*, recognizing his unparalleled impact) influenced the Circle of Growth's design as a *comprehensive system*. By stressing strategic planning, accountability, and aligning personal purpose with organizational goals, Drucker's work sharpened the Circle's guidance on leadership and operating structures. The *Circle of Growth* incorporates Drucker's lessons on focusing on results, adapting to change, and continually developing one's effectiveness as both an individual and a leader.

- **Charlie Munger** – Investor, philanthropist, and Warren Buffett's long-time business partner, Munger is revered for his *multi-disciplinary mental model* approach to decision-making. He advocates building a "latticework of mental models" – a toolkit of fundamental principles from economics, psychology, mathematics, biology, etc. – to make better decisions and avoid cognitive biases. Munger's wisdom (famously captured in *Poor Charlie's Almanack*) taught that understanding concepts like **opportunity cost, inversion**, and **regression to the mean**, among many others, leads to sound judgment in business and life. His approach of *worldly wisdom* influenced The Circle of Growth's emphasis on mindset and continuous learning. By encouraging individuals to think broadly across disciplines, challenge their own assumptions, and focus on long-term rationality over short-term emotion, Munger's principles help the Circle's users sharpen their decision-making and strategy. The Circle particularly embodies Munger's advice on cultivating *mental frameworks* (e.g. knowing one's **Circle of Competence**, avoiding confirmation bias, and seeking win-win outcomes), thereby grounding the system in robust, proven thinking models.

- **John Maynard Keynes** – A pioneering economist whose ideas shaped modern macroeconomics, Keynes also provided keen insight into investor psychology and capital markets. He popularized the term "*animal spirits*" to describe the emotions and instincts that drive economic decisions and market fluctuations. Keynes observed that waves of optimism and pessimism among investors can lead to booms and busts beyond what fundamentals justify, highlighting the role of psychology in financial systems. Not only a theorist, Keynes was a successful practitioner – managing the endowment for King's College, Cambridge, and achieving strong returns by exploiting market inefficiencies. He believed in profiting from others' irrationality, favoring a contrarian approach (for example, buying undervalued stocks when others were fearful) and he stressed the importance of *liquidity management and long-term outlook* in investingt.

Keynes's influence on The Circle of Growth appears in the system's awareness of economic cycles and behavioral economics: the framework encourages maintaining a balance between seizing opportunities during market downturns and holding reserves for stability. By crediting Keynes, the Circle underscores that sustainable prosperity requires understanding both the hard data **and** the "soft" human factors that move markets and economies.

- **Daniel Kahneman** – A Nobel Prize-winning psychologist, Kahneman (with colleague Amos Tversky) founded the field of *behavioral economics* by demonstrating how human decisions often stray from pure rationality. He introduced concepts of cognitive biases and heuristics – systematic thinking errors like **loss aversion**, **overconfidence**, and **confirmation bias** – which explain why individuals often misjudge risk and reward.. Kahneman's landmark *Prospect Theory* showed that people weigh losses more heavily than equivalent gains, fundamentally altering economic and financial theories of choice under uncertainty. His work (summarized for a broad audience in *Thinking, Fast and Slow*) taught the world that our minds use a fast, intuitive system prone to bias, and a slower, analytical system that requires effort. The Circle of Growth incorporates Kahneman's insights by encouraging *mindfulness and reflection in financial decisions*: it alerts readers to common pitfalls like impulsive reactions to market swings or short-term noise. By crediting Kahneman, the author's system highlights the importance of self-awareness and psychological resilience in wealth-building – training oneself to think critically, mitigate biases, and make choices that are logically sound rather than emotionally driven.

- **Objectives and Key Results (OKRs):** A goal-setting framework that links high-level *objectives* with a handful of specific, measurable *key results*. Originating at Intel under Andy Grove and later popularized by John Doerr at Google, OKRs help organizations and individuals set ambitious goals and track outcomes quantitatively. A typical OKR might state an Objective (e.g. "Improve our online customer experience") and 3–5 Key Results (concrete targets such as "Increase website conversion rate by 15% this quarter"). The **Circle of Growth** draws on OKR principles by urging readers to define clear goals in each area of growth and tie them to metrics – reinforcing alignment between one's vision and day-to-day actions. By using OKRs' blend of aspiration and accountability, the Circle's methodology ensures that progress can be measured and adjusted, teaching that *"what gets measured gets improved."* This framework sharpened the Circle by instilling a results-focused discipline: it's not enough to have dreams; one must also define how success will be recognized and attained.

- **Eisenhower Matrix (Urgent-Important Matrix):** A classic productivity and time-management tool that helps prioritize tasks by urgency and importance. Based on a concept attributed to U.S. President Dwight D. Eisenhower (and later popularized by Stephen Covey's teachings on time management), it divides activities into four quadrants: **Urgent & Important (Do first)**, **Important but Not Urgent (Schedule)**, **Urgent but Not Important (Delegate)**, and **Neither (Eliminate)**. This simple matrix guided the author in structuring the Circle of Growth's approach to time and energy management. By crediting the Eisenhower Matrix, the system emphasizes that *not all tasks are created equal* – long-term wealth and personal development come from consistently investing time in important-but-not-urgent activities (like planning, learning, and relationship-building) rather than getting lost in firefighting. The Circle of Growth incorporates this framework to coach readers on focusing on what truly moves the needle (strategic, high-value work) and having the discipline to defer or delegate distractions. In essence, the Eisenhower principle sharpened the Circle's guidance on productivity: encouraging proactive time allocation to priorities that compound growth, instead of reacting to every minor demand.

- **SMART Goals:** A widely used framework for effective goal-setting, ensuring that objectives are clearly defined and achievable. "SMART" stands for **Specific, Measurable, Achievable, Relevant, and Time-bound**. A SMART goal turns a vague ambition ("build wealth") into a precise target (e.g. "Save $10,000 by December 31 by automatically investing 15% of each paycheck"). The SMART criteria enforce clarity (what exactly to accomplish and why), concrete metrics to track progress, realism in scope, alignment with broader values, and a deadline to create urgency. In *Wealth Unlocked*, the Circle of Growth method credits the SMART framework for its influence on the "Comprehensive Growth Roadmap" and action plans. By using SMART goals, the system helps readers break down grand visions into manageable steps and milestones. This ensures that the journey to prosperity is not just inspirational but also executable. The SMART approach sharpened the Circle by instilling *focus and accountability* — every element of one's growth plan should be articulated in a way that progress can be measured and success clearly recognized, thereby dramatically increasing the odds of follow-through.

- **Pareto Principle (80/20 Rule):** The observation by economist Vilfredo Pareto that roughly 80% of outcomes stem from 20% of causes. In practice, this means a small fraction of activities often generate the majority of results. For example, 20% of a company's customers might produce 80% of the revenue, or focusing on the most critical 20% of your tasks may yield 80% of the benefit. This "law of the vital few" has become a cornerstone of modern productivity and strategic planning. The Circle of Growth adopts the 80/20 mindset to help users concentrate on high-impact actions in their finances and personal development. By identifying which habits, investments, or business strategies lie in that key 20% (the *critical few* that drive growth), the author's system encourages readers to double down on those and trim the rest. Acknowledging the Pareto Principle sharpened the Circle's efficiency: it teaches that *growth accelerates* when you eliminate trivial distractions and direct your effort to the areas that truly matter – a small set of smart choices, repeated consistently, can produce outsized rewards over time.

Each of the above thinkers, books, and frameworks contributed a vital piece to **The Circle of Growth** system. In assembling his signature framework, Theodore Schiele drew on the rich insights of financial teachers, leadership experts, economists, and strategists who came before – translating their wisdom into a cohesive model for personal prosperity. This References & Bibliography section, **"Thinkers, Operators, and Frameworks That Sharpened the Circle,"** gratefully acknowledges those influential ideas. Together, they form the intellectual foundation beneath *Wealth Unlocked*, ensuring that the guidance within is not only inspirational, but anchored in proven principles and timeless wisdom. The author encourages readers to explore these sources further, both to deepen their understanding and to continue the journey of learning that underlies all sustainable growth. Each reference is a reminder that *success leaves clues* – and The Circle of Growth is built upon the collective genius of many who have unlocked wealth and wisdom before.

Appendices (Field Kits)
Visual Diagrams

The 3 Growth Zones: *Comfort → Adversity → Growth.* A simple circle map that reminds you: safety feels good, adversity feels messy, growth feels earned.

The Growth Grid

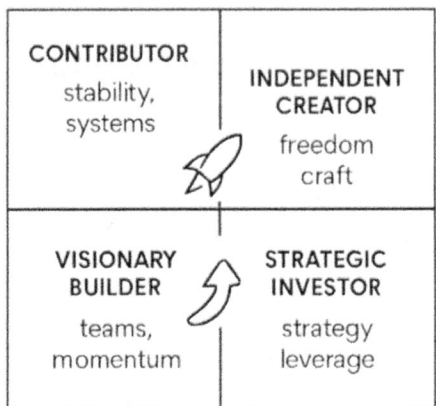

The Growth Grid: Contributor, Independent Creator, Visionary Builder, Strategic Investor. A clarity chart to help you identify your natural lane and design work that fits your wiring.

The Circle of Growth

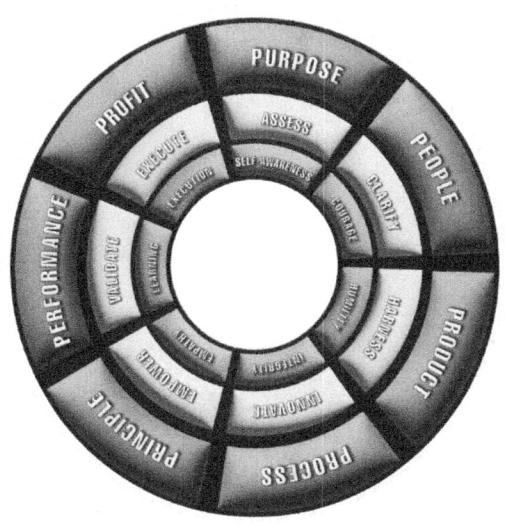

The **Circle of Growth** is a practical leadership operating system built on a continuous, repeatable cycle designed to drive sustainable personal and professional growth. It follows seven key stages — **Assess, Clarify, Harness, Innovate, Empower, Validate,** and **Execute** — forming a self-sustaining loop rather than a one-time climb. Each stage strengthens the next: assessing truth builds clarity, clarity harnesses focus, innovation fuels momentum, empowerment expands impact, validation ensures alignment, and execution delivers measurable results. The process repeats, creating a rhythm of learning, adaptation, and leadership mastery.

Personal Growth

Personal Growth is the ongoing process of becoming your best self through self-awareness, discipline, and intentional action. It's about assessing where you are, clarifying what matters most, and harnessing your energy toward meaningful change. Through consistent cycles of reflection, learning, and execution, personal growth transforms challenges into lessons and habits into mastery. It's not about perfection—it's about progress, purpose, and the courage to keep evolving.

Professional Development

Professional Development is the disciplined process of advancing your skills, mindset, and impact in your field through intentional learning and application. It's about assessing your current strengths, clarifying the areas for growth, and harnessing opportunities—like mentorship, collaboration, and feedback—to elevate your performance. True professional growth happens through consistent innovation, accountability, and refinement, where every project becomes a practice ground for leadership. It's not just about climbing a career ladder; it's about expanding your capacity to lead, contribute, and create lasting value.

The 7Ps

The Seven P's represent the essential framework for purposeful leadership and sustainable success. Together, they form a system that balances clarity, integrity, and execution. It begins with **Purpose**, the "why" that drives every action, supported by **People**, the relationships that fuel growth. **Product** and **Process** ensure quality and consistency, while **Principles** anchor you in values. **Performance** measures progress through discipline and learning, and **Profit** sustains your mission through meaningful results. When aligned, the Seven P's transform intention into impact—creating a rhythm of growth that endures.

S.U.M.

S.U.M. — System, Unity, and Mastery is a practical leadership model built on structure, collaboration, and excellence. *System* creates order and alignment, turning vision into actionable steps. *Unity* fosters teamwork and shared purpose, ensuring that people move together toward common goals. *Mastery* is the ongoing pursuit of growth—learning, refining, and leading by example. Together, these three elements form a rhythm of discipline, connection, and progress that transforms potential into lasting impact.

The Asset Navigator

The Circle of Growth — Overview

The Circle of Growth is a continuous cycle of development designed to help leaders and teams evolve with intention. It moves through seven core stages: **Assess, Clarify, Harness, Innovate, Empower, Validate, and Execute.** *Each step strengthens the next—helping you identify truth, align purpose, build systems, and act with confidence.*

Personal Growth

Weekly Scorecard
- Re-assess purpose
- Re-clarify 3-5 outcomes
- Re-harness resources
- Retire what failed

Journaling Prompts
- What did I learn this week about my habits or leadership?
- Where did I stay in my comfort zone, and where did I step into adversity?
- What decisions or actions moved me closer to growth?
- What do I need to clarify, delegate, or release next week?

Professional Development

Weekly Scorecard
- Re-assess purpose
- Re-clarify 3-5 outcomes
- Re-harness resources
- Retire what failed

Journaling Prompts
- Growth & Awareness
  What did I learn this week about my habits, decisions, or mindset as a leader?
- Challenge & Courage
  Where did I stretch beyond comfort — and what did that experience reveal about my resilience?
- Focus & Follow-Through
  What's one action I'll take next week to create measurable growth or clarity?

Workflow

Weekly Scorecard
- What mattered?
- What shipped?
- What's blocked?
- What's next? _____

Quarterly Scorecard
- What systems, routines, or relationships created real progress this quarter?
- Which goals or habits no longer serve my growth? Where did I see the greatest personal or professional return on effort?
- What 3-5 priorities will I commit to in the next quarter?

Step-by-Step Exercises

- *90-Day Quick Start:*
  - **Weeks 1–2**: Run *Assess + Clarify*. Name owners, define outcomes, set rhythms.
  - **Weeks 3–6**: *Harness + Innovate*. Align resources, run small bets, measure early wins.
  - **Weeks 7–12**: *Empower + Validate + Execute*. Delegate, measure, deliver, review.
- *The Comfort Breaker Drill*:

Pick one action you've been avoiding. Do it this week. Treat discomfort as training, not danger.

- ***The Adversity Reframe***:

Write down one rejection or setback. Next to it, note the lesson, the adjustment, and the new step. This shifts pain into progress.

- ***The Growth Grid Check-In***:

Every quarter, ask: Am I living in my true lane, or wearing a costume? Realignment beats burnout.

Glossary

A

- **Accountability:** Owning your actions and commitments, and being answerable for the results. It means no excuses – you take responsibility and follow through on what you promised.

- **Adversity Zone:** The challenging "messy middle" where setbacks and discomfort test your character and habits. Growth isn't easy here, but working through adversity builds strength and new skills.

- **Agile:** A project management method based on short cycles, quick feedback, and adaptability. Teams using Agile work in small sprints, learn fast, and adjust often instead of sticking to a rigid long-term plan.

- **Alignment:** Everyone pulling in the same direction. When a team or plan is in alignment, goals, actions, and values all support each other – people know the plan and their role in it, reducing friction.

- **Assess:** The first step of the Circle of Growth loop – take an honest look at where things stand. You gather facts, find the real baseline, note any risks, and clarify who's responsible for what. In short, start with a clear reality check before making a plan.

- **Asset Navigator:** A framework for shifting from being a hands-on builder to being an investor. It helps you map out how to build and manage assets (businesses, investments, etc.) in line with your values and the legacy you want to leave.

B

- **Buy-In:** Genuine agreement and commitment from everyone involved. When a team has buy-in, members understand the "why" behind a decision or plan and are personally invested in making it succeed.

C

- **Circle of Growth:** A leadership system that connects who you are (your character and values) with what you do (your actions) in a continuous, repeatable loop. Think of it as a cycle: clarity → action → results → adjustment → repeat – aligning personal growth with performance in a sustainable way.

- **Clarify:** Define the goals, outcomes, and roles. This step is about deciding exactly what "success" looks like and spelling out who will do what by when. Clarity beats chaos: everyone ends up on the same page about the target and their part in achieving it.

- **Collaboration:** Working jointly with others so that each person's contributions and strengths help achieve a common goal. True collaboration means sharing ideas openly, supporting each other, and solving problems together rather than in isolation.

- **Comfort Zone:** A safe but stagnant space of familiarity where you're not really challenged. Things feel easy here because they're routine, but you're not growing. Stepping out of the comfort zone is where improvement begins.

- **Commitment:** The act of fully dedicating to a decision, plan, or goal. In a team context, commitment means everyone sticks to the agreed course of action (even if it wasn't their first choice) and sees it through, instead of second-guessing or waffling.

- **Communication (Effective Communication):** Clear, two-way exchange of information. It means speaking in a way others understand and actively listening to others in return. Good communication leaves no room for harmful assumptions – everyone knows what's expected and feels heard.

- **Compounding:** The snowball effect where small, consistent wins or improvements build on each other over time to create big results. Like interest in a bank account, little gains compound into significant growth if you keep at it.

- **Conflict (Productive Conflict):** Openly addressing differences in opinions or approaches in a healthy, respectful way. Rather than avoiding issues or resorting to personal attacks, productive conflict means debating ideas frankly for the good of the team and finding the best solution.

- **Contributor:** In the Growth Grid, a person who loves structure, systems, and consistency. Contributors are the steady engines of a team – reliable and process-driven. They keep things organized and running smoothly, though they may prefer routine over big changes.

- **Courage:** Choosing to do what's right or needed even when it's uncomfortable or risky. It's having the guts to step out of your comfort zone, make a hard call, or try something new when others might shy away.

- **Culture:** The shared values, norms, and behaviors of your team or organization – essentially "how we do things here." A healthy culture encourages growth, trust, and accountability. It's felt in everyday interactions and decisions, setting the tone for the work environment.

D

- **Delegation:** Handing over responsibility and authority to someone else. Effective delegation means you entrust a task or decision to another person (providing guidance as needed) and allow them the ownership to get it done. This develops others and frees you to focus where you're most needed.

- **Discipline:** Consistent adherence to a standard or plan, even when it's tough or you don't feel like it. Discipline is doing what needs to be done, day in and day out. It's the habit behind execution – for example, sticking to a workout schedule or always closing out your daily tasks – that leads to long-term success.

E

- **Empathy:** The ability to understand and share someone else's feelings or perspective. In practice, empathy means seeing team members as people (not just "employees" or roles) and caring about what they're experiencing. It helps you respond with compassion and build trust, because people feel understood.

- **Empower:** Delegate with guardrails to build trust and confidence in others. When you empower someone, you give them ownership of their work along with the support and resources to succeed. It's saying, "I trust you to run with this," and meaning it – you let them find their way to the result, and you share the wins with them.

- **EOS (Entrepreneurial Operating System):** A practical business management framework popularized by the book *Traction* by Gino Wickman. EOS focuses on strengthening six key components of a business (like Vision, People, Data, Issues, Process, and Traction) through simple tools and routines, so that the organization is aligned and executes well.

- **Execute (Execution):** Finishing the plan and delivering results with consistency and discipline. To execute means to do what you said you would do, the way you said you'd do it – no half-done work or dropped balls. It's about seeing things through to completion reliably, and "closing the loop" on your goals.

- **Extreme Ownership:** A mindset of taking full responsibility for everything in your realm, whether or not it's directly your fault. In practice, it means no blaming or finger-pointing – if something goes wrong, you own the problem and work to fix it.

This level of responsibility creates a culture of trust and action, because everyone is focused on solutions rather than excuses.

F

- **Feedback:** Information or reactions about performance or behavior given to help someone improve. Good feedback is timely and specific – it highlights what's working, what isn't, and why. In a healthy team, feedback goes both ways (up, down, and across), and it's about learning, not punishing.

- **Fixed Mindset:** The belief that abilities and intelligence are set in stone (you "have it or you don't"). With a fixed mindset, people tend to avoid challenges and fear failure, thinking it will make them look inadequate. This is the opposite of a growth mindset – it can limit learning because you assume you can't change.

- **Flywheel:** A metaphor for building momentum. A flywheel is a heavy wheel that's hard to start turning, but once it's spinning, it generates its own energy and keeps going. In leadership or business, a flywheel effect is when your consistent efforts start compounding – each success makes the next success easier, and over time you achieve accelerating growth or progress.

G

- **Goals:** Clear targets or outcomes you aim to achieve. Goals give you and your team focus and something to measure progress against. Strong goals are specific and measurable (think SMART goals or OKRs), so you know exactly what you're shooting for and when you've hit the mark.

- **Grit:** A mix of passion and perseverance for long-term goals. Someone with grit keeps pushing through setbacks and boredom because they care deeply about the end goal. It's that stick-with-it-ness – you don't quit when things get hard, and over time that persistence pays off.

- **Growth Grid:** A framework that identifies four natural "lanes" or approaches people take in their growth and work. These lanes are Contributor, Independent Creator, Visionary Builder, and Strategic Investor. Knowing your place on the Growth Grid helps you understand your strengths and preferences in how you lead and get things done.

- **Growth Mindset:** The belief that abilities and intelligence can be developed through effort, learning, and feedback. With a growth mindset, you see challenges as opportunities to grow rather than threats. You're more likely to embrace learning, persist through obstacles, and ultimately improve over time (as opposed to a fixed mindset).

H

- **Habits:** Regular practices or routines that shape your behavior. Good habits (like writing down daily priorities or exercising each morning) build momentum and discipline over time – they make positive actions almost automatic. In the Circle of Growth, building the right habits can turn one-time actions into lasting growth.

- **Harness:** Align people, time, and tools toward one priority. This step is about focus – you concentrate your team and resources on what matters most right now. Harnessing means cutting out the busywork or nice-to-haves and making sure everyone and everything is pointed in the same direction to maximize impact.

- **Humility:** Staying grounded and teachable. Humility in leadership means you don't assume you have all the answers – you listen to others, admit when you're wrong or don't know something, and let the best ideas rise (even if they're not yours). It's about confidence without arrogance.

I

- **Implementer:** A person who excels at turning plans into reality through organization and detail. The implementer is a structured doer – their strength is execution (they make sure things actually get done). The risk for an implementer is getting so caught up in managing tasks that they might lose sight of the bigger picture or new opportunities.

- **Independent Creator:** Someone who values freedom, originality, and personal ownership of their work. Independent creators like to have control over outcomes that tie directly to their own effort. They thrive when they can put their personal stamp on projects and often prefer working on their own or with minimal oversight.

- **Innovate:** Find a smarter, better way to do the work. To innovate is to improve or solve problems creatively – maybe by simplifying a process, trying a new method, or using a new tool. The key is doing it in line with your values and mission (no cheating or cutting corners on integrity). Big or small, innovation is about continuously getting better rather than sticking with "how we've always done it."

- **Integrity:** Doing the right thing even when it's inconvenient or no one's watching. A person with integrity keeps their promises and sticks to their values – they choose honesty and ethics over easy wins. In a team, integrity builds trust: people know you'll act honorably and transparently.

- **iPerson:** A self-focused, ego-driven person who avoids accountability and growth. Think "it's all about me." An iPerson's default is to protect their ego – they deflect blame, resist feedback, and care more about looking good or being right than improving or helping the team. (In the Circle of Growth, this is the trap to avoid.)

- **IPS (Investment Policy Statement):** A one-page plan for how you'll invest your money or resources. An IPS typically lays out your goals, what risks you're willing to take, the rules or principles you'll follow, and your process for making decisions. It's like a personal guide to ensure your investments align with your objectives and values.

L

- **Lean:** A system for working efficiently by continuously eliminating waste and improving processes. Originating from manufacturing (think Toyota), Lean is about doing more with less – constantly refining how work gets done so there's no excess cost, effort, or materials, and quality stays high.

- **Learning:** Staying teachable and adaptable. Embracing learning means acknowledging you don't know everything and actively seeking to grow your skills and knowledge. When you have a learning mindset, setbacks don't defeat you – they educate you. You ask for feedback, learn from others, and keep improving.

- **Legacy:** The lasting impact of your work and leadership, measured in how it lives on after you. Your legacy is what you build today that endures – the values you instill, the systems you create, the lives you touch. A legacy-driven leader thinks beyond short-term results and considers how their choices will benefit others in the long run, even when they're not around.

M

- **Mastery:** Deep, thorough expertise in something achieved through continuous improvement and practice. Mastery isn't an overnight thing – it's when you've honed a skill or craft so well that it looks almost effortless. In a growth context, it's the pursuit of ever-higher levels of skill and understanding.

- **Mindset:** Your collection of attitudes or beliefs that shapes how you see the world and respond to it. In a leadership context, mindset influences everything – whether you see challenges as opportunities or threats, how you handle criticism, and if you believe you (and others) can grow. Cultivating a positive, growth-oriented mindset sets the tone for success.

- **Mission:** The core purpose or big "why" of an organization or individual. A mission defines what you're here to do and for whom – it's the fundamental goal or problem you exist to address. Think of it as your guiding star for day-to-day decisions, ensuring your work has direction and meaning.

O

- **OKRs (Objectives and Key Results):** A goal-setting framework used by many successful companies (like Google). It works by defining a big Objective (the what/where you want to go) and 3-5 measurable Key Results (how you know you're making progress toward that objective). OKRs create clarity and focus, and they're usually set and reviewed in short cycles (quarterly, for example).

- **Operating Rhythm (Cadence):** A consistent, repeatable schedule of activities that keeps your team in sync and on track. This could be your regular meeting schedule, planning cycles, check-ins, or other routines. An effective operating rhythm creates a steady drumbeat for the organization – everyone knows when key things happen and can march together.

- **Operating System (Leadership OS):** The underlying framework or "way of working" you use to run your team or organization, much like a computer's operating system runs a computer. It's the set of leadership habits, processes, and tools that everything else runs on. A good leadership OS brings consistency and efficiency to decision-making, communication, and execution.

- **Organizational Health:** The overall well-being and functioning of an organization. It's about more than just hitting targets – it includes the quality of the culture, the level of trust, how effectively people communicate, and how resilient the team is. A healthy organization has clear alignment, open communication, high trust, and a culture that allows people and strategies to thrive.

- **Ownership:** The attitude of taking initiative and responsibility for outcomes as if you "own" the result. Someone with ownership doesn't wait to be told – they step up, solve problems, and take pride in the outcome (good or bad). It's closely tied to accountability, but it's more of a personal mindset of care and initiative: you treat the business or project like it's yours.

P

- **Pareto Principle (80/20 Rule):** The idea that roughly 20% of the inputs or activities produce about 80% of the outcomes. In practice, it means a few things are responsible for most results – so focus on those critical few. For example, a business might find that 20% of its customers drive 80% of sales. Using the 80/20 rule helps prioritize high-impact tasks over busywork.

- **People:** In the Circle of Growth's "7 Ps," this refers to who you're working with and the quality of those relationships. Focusing on People means having the right teammates and investing in trust, collaboration, and communication. It's recognizing that **who** is on the journey with you matters for success.

- **Performance:** One of the "7 Ps," focused on how success is measured. Performance is about the key metrics and results that show whether you're making progress. It answers, "How do we know we're winning?" Keeping an eye on performance ensures that effort turns into tangible outcomes and that you can celebrate wins or spot issues early.

- **Principles:** Guiding values or rules (another of the 7 Ps) that inform how decisions are made and how work gets done. Principles are your non-negotiables – the core beliefs that everyone on the team understands. For instance, a principle could be "customer first" or "quality over speed." When principles are clear, they act like a compass during tough decisions.

- **Process:** The "how" in the 7 Ps – it's the series of steps or the system for getting work done. A good process is efficient and clear, so work flows smoothly from start to finish. When you focus on Process, you map out who does what, in what order, and how to avoid waste or confusion along the way.

- **Product:** In the 7 Ps, this refers to what value you're creating or delivering. Your "product" could be a physical item, a service, or a specific outcome or project. It's the **what** that all your efforts are building. Clarity about the Product ensures everyone knows the end deliverable and the value it's supposed to provide.

- **Profit:** One of the 7 Ps, pointing to the sustainable gains from your efforts. Profit can mean financial gain, but in a broader leadership sense it can also mean the surplus of trust, goodwill, or impact you earn. It's the benefit that you can reinvest – money to grow the business, credibility to take on bigger projects, or momentum to keep improving.

- **Psychological Safety:** A team environment where everyone feels safe to speak up, ask questions, and take smart risks without fear of being punished or ridiculed. In a psychologically safe culture, people know they won't be embarrassed or penalized for admitting a mistake or saying "I don't know." This safety is key for innovation and honest communication, because it encourages people to contribute ideas and surface problems early.

- **Purpose:** The "why" behind what you're doing (and one of the key 7 Ps). Purpose is your mission or reason for existing boiled down to a clear statement of meaning. It gives direction and motivation – when everyone knows **why** their work matters, it's easier to push through challenges and make decisions that align with that greater goal.

R

- **Resilience:** The ability to bounce back from setbacks, adapt, and keep going. A resilient person (or team) handles adversity without losing motivation or optimism for long. Instead of giving up after a failure or shock, resilience means you learn from it, adjust, and come back stronger.

S

- **S.U.M. (System, Unity, Mastery):** A framework for scaling leadership into your team's culture by focusing on three elements. **System** means setting up structures and rewards so the **team** (not just individuals) wins together. **Unity** means creating regular rhythms and practices that keep the whole team aligned and moving as one. **Mastery** means encouraging everyone to share knowledge and continuously develop skills so no one person becomes a single point of failure. In short, S.U.M. helps a leader multiply their impact by turning personal leadership into a team-wide strength.

- **Scalable Growth:** Growth that sticks and can be repeated over time, not just a one-time spike. It's like building a strong foundation rather than chasing a quick high. When growth is scalable, you can sustain it and build on it – your systems and habits make sure today's success can lead to more success tomorrow.

- **Self-Awareness:** Knowing yourself – your strengths, weaknesses, habits, and how your behavior impacts others. Self-awareness means being honest about your blind spots and triggers. The benefit: when you understand yourself, you can lead yourself (and others) much more effectively, adjusting your approach as needed.

- **Strategic Investor:** One of the Growth Grid lanes – a person who plays the long game to create value. Strategic investors focus on building assets, wealth, and systems that generate opportunities for others over time. They think in terms of sustainability and legacy: rather than day-to-day operations, they're looking at how to invest resources for future growth and impact.

- **Systems Thinking:** Looking at a situation or organization as a whole system with interrelated parts, rather than just reacting to individual events. Someone practicing systems thinking understands that changing one part of the system can affect other parts. This approach helps in finding root causes of problems and designing solutions that improve the entire process (not just a single point). It's the opposite of a siloed or short-sighted view – it's about seeing the big picture and the connections.

T

- **Teamwork:** People working together effectively toward a shared goal. Good teamwork means members communicate, trust each other, and combine their strengths. In a strong team, everyone pulls their weight and has each other's backs – the group achieves more together than the individuals could on their own.

- **Traction:** Real, tangible forward progress – like a car tire finally gripping the road and moving forward. In a business or project, getting traction means your efforts are taking hold and producing results (instead of spinning in place). It's the feeling of momentum: plans turning into action, and action turning into consistent wins.

- **Transparency:** Openness and honesty in how you work and communicate. A transparent leader or organization shares information freely (when appropriate), so people aren't kept in the dark. Transparency builds trust – when folks know the why and what of decisions or see data openly, they feel respected and can engage more fully. It's basically "no hidden agendas."

- **Trust:** Confidence in the integrity and reliability of others. In a team setting, trust means you believe your teammates will do what they say they'll do and look out for the group's best interests. Trust is the backbone of teamwork – when it's there, people feel safe to take initiative or risks, and communication flows freely. Without trust, teams fall into blame and fear.

U

- **Unity:** A sense of togetherness and common purpose in a team. Unity means everyone is on the same page and has each other's back – "we win or lose together." When a team has unity, there's little infighting or silo mentality; instead, people prioritize the collective goal over individual agendas.

V

- **Validate:** Check the results and learn from them. To validate is to ask "Is it working? Prove it," and then look at real evidence (data, feedback, metrics) to answer that. This step ensures you measure progress against your expected outcomes. By validating, you catch successes to celebrate and problems to fix – it turns guesswork into learning, so you can make informed adjustments.

- **Vision:** A clear picture of the future you want to create. A vision describes an inspiring end-state – what things will look like if you succeed at your mission. It gives direction and hope, rallying people because they see the destination that all their efforts are moving toward.

- **Visionary:** A big-picture thinker who sees possibilities and ideas that aren't reality yet. Visionaries are great at imagining the future and coming up with creative concepts. Their strength is inspiration and direction through ideas, but their risk is getting lost in dreaming without executing those ideas. (They often need implementers to help make visions real.)

- **Visionary Builder:** A role in the Growth Grid – this person not only envisions big ideas but also builds the structure or organization to achieve them. Visionary Builders see the big picture **and** know how to organize people and resources to create scale. They're the entrepreneurs and leaders who take a vision and construct something tangible and scalable from it.

- **Vulnerability:** The courage to show your authentic self – including your weaknesses, fears, or mistakes. In leadership, vulnerability means being honest and open (for example, admitting "I was wrong" or "I need help" when necessary). It's not a weakness; it builds trust and encourages others to be open as well. When leaders are vulnerable, it creates a safe space for everyone to learn and grow.

Z

- **Zone of Growth:** The stage or space where real development happens – you're past the comfort zone and have navigated adversity, and now your consistent efforts start to pay off. In the Zone of Growth, you're seeing evidence of improvement, gaining confidence, and building momentum. It's where hard-earned lessons turn into legacy and lasting success, as your good habits compound into great results.

Book Club & Leadership Circle Discussion Questions

Discussion Prompts for *The Circle of Growth*

The Seven Actions of the Growth Loop

- The Growth Loop is built on seven key actions – **Assess, Clarify, Harness, Innovate, Empower, Validate, and Execute**. Which of these actions comes most naturally to you, and which one do you find the most challenging to practice consistently? How have these strengths or gaps shown up in your leadership so far?

- **Assess** means starting with the truth – getting a clear baseline of reality (facts, risks, assumptions) before taking action. Can you share a time when taking the time to assess a situation upfront made a difference in the outcome, or a time when skipping an honest assessment led to problems later on? What did you learn from that experience about the value of **pausing to get clarity**?

- **Empower** is about trusting your people and *delegating with guardrails* instead of trying to do everything yourself. How do you decide what responsibilities to hand off to others on your team, and what tends to hold you back from delegating more? What's one task you handle now that you could empower someone else to take on as a growth opportunity for them?

The Seven Traits (Who You Are as a Leader)

- *The Circle of Growth* highlights seven core leadership traits – **Self-Awareness, Courage, Humility, Integrity, Empathy, Learning, and Execution**. Which of these traits would you call your personal superpower, and which one do you feel you need to develop further? How have your strongest trait (and your weakest) each impacted your team's performance or your own effectiveness?

- Think of a time when one of these traits was **put to the test** in your leadership (for example, when your Courage or Empathy was challenged by a tough situation). What happened, and how did staying true to (or straying from) that trait affect the outcome and the people involved? What does that story tell you about the importance of that trait in leadership?

- The book emphasizes linking *"who we are" (traits) with "what we do" (actions)*. Can you share an example of a leader (perhaps yourself or someone you admire) whose personal character – say, their integrity or humility – directly shaped a decision or outcome for the team? How have you seen a leader's values translate into practical results or culture in the workplace?

The Growth Grid (Finding Your Natural Lane)

- *The Growth Grid* identifies four natural leadership "lanes": **Contributor, Independent Creator, Visionary Builder,** and **Strategic Investor**. Which of these lanes do you feel best describes you at this stage of your career, and why? What daily activities or personal strengths make you feel that you're in that lane?

- Have you ever found yourself **"wearing a costume"** in a role that didn't fit your natural lane? How did that misalignment impact your performance or well-being (e.g. feeling burned out or underutilized), and what did you learn from that experience? In hindsight, how did it influence the way you now seek roles or structure your team to better fit people's natural strengths?

- If you wanted to **"stop forcing a life that doesn't fit and start building one that does"**, what is one practical change you could make in your current work to better align with your natural style? For example, could you delegate more, take on different responsibilities, or adjust your goals to play to your strengths? What positive outcome would you hope to see from that change in terms of your performance or growth?

Adversity to Growth Model (Comfort Zone → Adversity Zone → Growth Zone)

- *The Circle of Growth* describes a journey through three zones: the **Comfort Zone**, the **Adversity Zone**, and the **Zone of Growth**. Thinking about your current situation or a recent challenge, which zone do you feel you're in right now, and why? How does being in that zone feel in terms of stress, uncertainty, or excitement for you?

- Recall a significant setback or adversity you've faced in your leadership journey. How did you respond at first, and what lesson or positive outcome eventually came from that experience? In hindsight, what was the **"payoff" from that pain** – for example, a new insight, skill, or habit you gained – and how has it changed your approach to challenges now?

- The book says **"the Adversity Zone isn't here to end you; it's here to edit you"**. In what ways have the challenges you've faced **edited or changed you** as a leader? For instance, did a difficulty reshape your priorities, build a new habit, or alter your leadership style for the better? How will you make sure those hard-earned improvements stick as you continue to grow?

The Seven Ps (Key Focus Areas of the System)

- The Circle of Growth framework ties its habits to **Seven Ps** of business: **Purpose, People, Product, Process, Principles, Performance,** and **Profit**. In your current leadership context, which of these areas gets the most of your attention and energy, and which one do you suspect you might be overlooking? How might refocusing a bit more on the area you tend to neglect benefit your team or organization in the long run?

- Share an example from your experience where *focusing on one of the Seven Ps paid off*. For instance, was there a project that succeeded because the team got crystal clear on its **Purpose**, or a time when improving a **Process** issue led to a big performance gain? What happened, and what does that story teach you about how these elements (Purpose, People, Process, etc.) work together in driving growth?

- Sometimes **Principles** (your values and ethics) can clash with short-term **Performance or Profit** pressures. Have you ever faced a decision where you had to choose between sticking to your principles and hitting a specific target or financial goal? What did you decide, and what did you learn from the outcome about balancing doing what's right with delivering results?

The S.U.M. Culture Model (Scaling Up: System, Unity, Mastery)

- **S.U.M.** stands for **System, Unity, Mastery** – a model for turning your personal leadership habits into a strong team culture. **System** is about embedding your leadership practices into the structures and processes of the organization so things run smoothly even when you're not micromanaging. What is one process or "system" you could put in place to make your team more self-sufficient or aligned? How do you think that structural change would improve your team's performance or trust?

- **Unity** represents trust, collaboration, and a shared sense of purpose on the team. How do you currently cultivate unity so that people feel "in it together" rather than isolated or in silos? Describe a practice or team ritual you've used (or seen) that helped build genuine trust and camaraderie. Why do you think it was effective in bringing people together?

- **Mastery** is about continuous learning and excellence. What do you do to encourage a culture of mastery on your team, where everyone is always improving their skills and knowledge? Can you give an example of a time when investing in someone's development – through mentoring, training, or new challenges – paid off in their performance or confidence? How did that impact the team as a whole?

The Asset Navigator Framework (From Builder to Investor)

- The **Asset Navigator** framework helps a leader shift from being a hands-on business builder to becoming a strategic investor, aligning their wealth strategy with their values and legacy. If you wrote a simple "investment policy" for how you allocate your own resources (time, money, or expertise) toward growth, what would be one guiding principle in it? In other words, what values would you ensure your investments (whether in projects, people, or financial assets) always reflect?

- Transitioning to an investor or mentor mindset often means **letting go of control** over the day-to-day. What aspects of giving up direct control do you find most challenging as you step into a higher-level leadership or ownership role? How might clarifying your long-term *Purpose* or "why" help you overcome those challenges and trust others with important responsibilities? Can you envision a future role for yourself where you focus more on guiding and investing in others, rather than managing every detail?

Acknowledgments

First and foremost, I want to thank my father, **Theodore Roosevelt Schiele**. Dad, you laid the foundation for everything in this book. Your unwavering values, hard work, and quiet wisdom inspired the very concept of the *Circle of Growth*. I watched you turn challenges into opportunities through discipline and faith. Without your example lighting my way, this framework might never have taken shape. I hope this book serves as a love letter to the lessons you instilled in me.

I also want to thank **Mr. Buck**, an extraordinary teacher (who started as a substitute in my life but became so much more). Mr. Buck, you gave me the tough love I needed as a teenager in Ferriday. You told me straight to stop feeling sorry for myself and to work hard if I ever wanted to get out of our small town. That wake-up call changed my trajectory. I am grateful for your candor and belief that I could do better—because of you, I did do better.

I'm grateful to **Howard Jackson** and **Leo Graham** for showing me what leadership in action truly looks like. In different ways, each of you taught me that leadership isn't about titles or ranks; it's about how you treat people and step up when it counts. Watching you lead with integrity, courage, and consistency gave me a living example to follow. You both modeled the kind of servant leadership that I strive to emulate every day. Thank you for demonstrating how to lead by doing.

I am indebted to **1SG Sam Smith**, my very first leader in uniform. First Sergeant Smith, you set the bar high from day one. You showed me how discipline, duty, and genuine care for your soldiers can earn respect without ever raising your voice. The lessons I learned under your guidance—about accountability, teamwork, and perseverance—have stayed with me through every chapter of my life. Thank you for being the leader I needed as a young soldier finding his way.

I must also acknowledge **CSM Sapp**, who taught me an invaluable lesson in how to teach and lead others. Command

Sergeant Major Sapp, you introduced me to a method that I carry with me to this day: *"Name it, explain it, demonstrate it, let them do practical work, and then take ownership."* This simple step-by-step approach to developing others has become a cornerstone of how I coach and mentor. You not only instructed me in that method, you lived it—ensuring I understood tasks, watched how to do them right, practiced them myself, and then owned the results. That approach gave me confidence and competence when I needed it most. I'm deeply grateful for your patience and for drilling into me a philosophy of leadership that multiplies itself through others.

Outside of my military family, I have been blessed with other mentors. I want to thank my father-in-law, who exemplified relentless productivity every single day. Watching you, I learned the value of an unwavering work ethic and the art of making the most of every hour. Your example showed me that consistent effort, even more than bursts of genius, is what builds a legacy. I also owe a special thanks to **David McLennan**, who devoted an entire year to mentoring me. David, you took me under your wing and taught me so much about business and leadership. You introduced me to EOS (the Entrepreneurial Operating System) and the B-I Triangle, and you fundamentally changed how I think operationally. Because of your guidance, I learned to see businesses as systems and to think strategically rather than just tactically. I wouldn't be the leader or the businessman I am today without your patient teaching. Thank you for pouring your time and wisdom into me—it made a world of difference.

Perhaps surprisingly, I want to extend my gratitude to all the people who overlooked or doubted me—especially those who did so when I retired from the military in 2019. To the ones who didn't see my potential or dismissed my mindset for success, thank you. Your skepticism became fuel for my fire.

Every time someone underestimated me, it only sharpened my resolve to prove what I was capable of. In a way, your doubt was a gift: it pushed me to work harder, stay humble, and demonstrate that success is something you carry inside long before anyone else can see it. I'm grateful for those skeptics and naysayers for unknowingly motivating me to be better and stronger.

I am also thankful for the hard moments and failures that have shaped me. In high school, being voted "least likely to succeed" felt like a punch in the gut at the time, but it turned out to be one of my greatest motivators. That indignity lit a fire in me to rewrite my story and show that labels don't define us—our drive and our heart do. Likewise, I've stumbled and failed more times than I can count—whether in business ventures that didn't pan out or personal mistakes that hurt people I cared about. Each failure, no matter how painful, taught me to take ownership of my shortcomings instead of making excuses. Failing (again and again) taught me humility. It taught me to be accountable for my actions and to learn and grow from every misstep. For all those lessons born from failure, I am grateful. They forced me to evolve when it would have been easier to quit.

One of the lowest points in my life was losing my apartment and becoming homeless during my senior year of college. At the time, it felt like the world was ending—I was embarrassed, frightened, and unsure of my future. Yet, in hindsight, I thank God for that season of struggle. Being without a home, even for a short while, taught me resilience in a way nothing else could. It made me resourceful and proved to me that I could survive and rebuild from absolutely nothing. I learned to be grateful for every small blessing—a hot meal, a friend's couch, a chance to keep studying—and I carried that gratitude forward. That experience hardened my resolve to never be in that situation again, but also softened my heart toward others facing hard times. It was a cruel teacher, but a thorough one, and I'm better for having lived through it.

Likewise, learning from failed relationships has been one of my most important teachers. It's easy to point fingers when things fall apart, but I learned that real growth begins when you take full responsibility for your part—no matter how uncomfortable that truth may be. Every relationship, whether it ended quietly or painfully, revealed something about who I was, what I valued, and where I needed to grow. Those experiences humbled me. They taught me to listen more deeply, communicate more clearly, and love more selflessly. I'm grateful for the lessons those chapters offered me, and I carry them forward as reminders that accountability is the gateway to becoming a better man.

In the end, every person mentioned here and every hardship endured has become part of my story—a story of growth, resilience, and purpose. I live the *Circle of Growth* daily; it's not just a framework in this book, but a way of life I embrace. Every day I push myself to step outside my comfort zone, just as so many of you taught me, because I know that's where real growth happens. If I preach anything in these pages, please know that I strive to practice it in my life.

To everyone—those named above and the many others who offered a helping hand, a word of advice, a lesson, or even a well-timed doubt—thank you. You have all contributed to my journey in profound ways. I carry your lessons and support with me in everything I do. This book is possible because of you. My hope is that the work I do and the legacy I build will honor the influence you've had on my life. From the bottom of my heart, thank you for believing in me (even when belief was hard), for challenging me, and for helping me unlock the wealth of lessons that I now eagerly share with others. I am forever grateful.

Thank you humbly for stepping into **the Circle of Growth** for choosing yourself, your evolution, and your truth. It's been an honor to support you on this part of your journey. May you continue to grow with courage, lead with clarity, and walk your path with pride. With respect and continued growth,

Theodore *Teddy Bear* Schiele, MSLM

Personal Website: www.BearSchiele.com

Business Website: www.Schiele.Group/

What I teach: www.Circle-of-Growth.com/

| Veteran | Visionary | Voice of Leadership |

Made in the USA
Coppell, TX
20 December 2025

64690214R00134